To Cade
Grandma &
Papa
Christmas 2013

CONTENTS.

CHAPTER		PAGE
I.	Old Virginia	7
II.	A Virginia Plantation	14
III.	The Boyhood of Washington	21
IV.	School-Days	29
V.	Mount Vernon and Belvoir	37
VI.	The Young Surveyor	45
VII.	The Ohio Company	52
VIII.	Major Washington	60
IX.	Fort Duquesne and Fort Necessity	70
X.	A Terrible Lesson in War	80
XI.	Commander-in-Chief of the Virginia Forces	95
XII.	Washington at Mount Vernon	107
XIII.	A Virginia Burgess	119
XIV.	The Continental Congress	131
XV.	Under the Old Elm	144
XVI.	Leading the Army	156
XVII.	At Valley Forge	170
XVIII.	The Conway Cabal	178
XIX.	Monmouth	187
XX.	The Last Campaign	194
XXI.	Washington resigns his Commission	203
XXII.	Mr. Washington	212
XXIII.	Called to the Helm	219
XXIV.	President Washington	226
XXV.	The Farewell	242

GEORGE WASHINGTON.

AN HISTORICAL BIOGRAPHY.

CHAPTER I.

OLD VIRGINIA.

IN 1732, when people spoke of Virginia, they meant commonly so much of the present State as lies between Chesapeake Bay and the Blue Ridge Mountains. In the valley of the Shenandoah River, just beyond the first range of mountains, there were a few families, chiefly Irish and German, who had made their way southward from Pennsylvania; the governor of Virginia, too, was at this time engaged in planting a colony of Germans in the valley. Still farther to the westward were a few bold pioneers, who built their log-cabins in the wilderness and lived by hunting and fishing. No one knew how far Virginia stretched; the old charters from the king had talked vaguely about the South Sea, meaning by that the Pacific Ocean; but the country beyond the mountains had never been surveyed, and scarcely even explored. The people who called themselves

Virginians looked upon those who lived beyond the Blue Ridge very much as nowadays persons on the Atlantic coast look upon those who settle in Dakota or Montana.

Down from these mountains came the streams which swelled into rivers, — the Potomac, the Rappahannock, the York, and the James, with their countless branches and runs and creeks. Look at any map of eastern Virginia and see what a long coast line it has, what arms of the sea stretch inland, what rivers come down to meet the sea, and what a net-work of water-ways spreads over the whole country. You would say that the people living there must be skillful fishermen and sailors, that thriving seaport towns would be scattered along the coast and rivers, and that there would be great shipyards for the building of all kinds of vessels.

But in 1732 there were no large towns in Virginia — there were scarcely any towns at all. Each county had a county seat, where were a court-house and a prison, and an inn for the convenience of those who had business in court; usually there was a church, and sometimes a small country store; but there were no other houses, and often the place was in the middle of the woods. The capital of Virginia — Williamsburg — had less than two hundred houses; and Norfolk, the largest town, at the head of a noble harbor, had a population of five thousand or so. A few fish were caught in the rivers or on the coast, but there was no business of fishing; a few boats plied from place to place, but there was no ship-building; and the ships which sailed into the harbors and up the rivers were owned elsewhere, and came from England or the other American colonies. There were no manufactures, and scarcely a trained mechanic in the whole colony. Yet Virginia was the most populous, and, some thought, the richest of the British colonies in America. In 1732 she had half a million inhabitants, — more than twice as many as New York had at that time.

Where were the people, then, and what were they doing? They were living in the country, and raising tobacco. More than a hundred years before, the first Englishmen who had come to Virginia had found that they could raise nothing which was so much wanted in England, and could bring them so much money, as tobacco. Besides, these Englishmen had not been mechanics or fishermen or sailors in England; they had for the most part been used to living on farms. So they fell at once to planting tobacco, and they could not raise enough to satisfy people in England and other parts of the Old World. All the fine gentlemen took to smoking; it was something new and fashionable; and, I suppose, a great many puffed away at their pipes who wondered what the pleasure was, and sometimes wished the weed had never been discovered. The king of England did not like it, and he wrote a book to dissuade people from the use of tobacco; but every one went on smoking Virginia tobacco as before.

The company which sent colonists to Virginia promised fifty acres to any one who would clear the land and settle upon it; for a small sum of money one might buy a hundred acres; and if any one did some special service to the colony, he might receive a gift of as much as two thousand acres. Now, in England, to own land was to be thought much of. Only noblemen or country gentlemen could boast of having two thousand or a hundred or even fifty acres. So the Englishmen who came to Virginia, where land was plenty, were all eager to own great estates.

To carry on such estates, and especially to raise tobacco, required many laborers. It was not easy for the Virginia land-owners to bring these from English farms. They could not be spared by the farmers there, and besides, such laborers were for the most part men and women who had never been beyond the villages where they had been born and had hardly ever heard of America. They lived, father and son, in the same place, and knew little about any other. But in London and other cities of England there were, at the time when the Virginia colony was formed, many poor people who had no work and nothing to live on. If these people could be sent to America, not only would the cities be rid of them, but the gentlemen in the new country would have laborers to cut down trees, clear the fields, and plant tobacco.

Accordingly, many of these idle and poor people were sent over as servants. The Virginia planters paid their passage, sheltered, fed, and clothed them, and in return had the use of their labor for a certain number of years. The plan did not work very well, however. Often these "indentured servants," as they were called, were idle and unwilling to work — that was one reason that they had been poor in London. Even when they did work, they were only " bound " for a certain length of time. After they had served their time, they were free. Then they sometimes cleared farms for themselves; but very often they led lazy, vicious lives, and were a trouble and vexation to the neighborhood.

It seemed to these Virginia planters that there was a better way. In 1619, a year before the Pilgrims landed at Plymouth, a Dutch captain brought up the James River twenty blacks whom he had captured on the coast of Africa. He offered to sell these to the planters, and they bought them. No one saw anything out of the way in this. It was no new thing to own slaves. There were slaves in the West India Islands, and in the countries of Europe. Indians when captured in war were sold into slavery. For that matter, white men had been made slaves. The difference between these blacks and the indentured servants was that the planter who paid the Dutch captain for a black man had the use of him all his lifetime, but if he bought from an English captain the services of an indentured white man, he could only have those services for a few months or years. It certainly was much more convenient to have an African slave.

There were not many of these slaves at first. An occasional shipload was brought from Africa, but it was not until after fifty years that negroes made any considerable part of the population. They had families, and all the children were slaves like their parents. More were bought of captains who made a business of going to Africa to trade for slaves, just as they might have gone to the East Indies for spices. The plantations were growing larger, and the more slaves a man had, the more tobacco he could raise; the more tobacco he could raise, the richer he was. Until long after the year 1732, the people in Virginia were wont to reckon the cost of things, not by pounds, shillings, and pence — the English currency, — but by pounds of tobacco — the Virginia currency. The salaries of the clergy were paid in tobacco; so were all their fees for christening, marrying, and burying. Taxes were paid and accounts were kept in tobacco. At a few points there were houses to which planters brought their tobacco, and these warehouses served the purpose of banks. A planter stored his tobacco and received a certificate of deposit. This certificate he could use instead of a check on a bank.

The small planters who lived high up the rivers, beyond the point where vessels could go, floated their tobacco in boats down to one of the warehouses, where it made part of the cargo of some ship sailing for England. But the largest part of this produce was shipped directly from the great plantations. Each of these had its own storehouse and its own wharf. The Virginia planter was his own shipping merchant. He had his agent in London. Once a year, a vessel would make its way up the river to his wharf. It brought whatever he or his family needed. He had sent to his agent to buy clothes, furniture, table-linen, tools, medicine, spices, foreign fruits, harnesses, carriages, cutlery, wines, books, pictures, — there was scarcely an article used in his house or on his plantation for which he did not send to London. Then in return he helped to load the vessel, and he had just one article with which to make up the cargo — tobacco. Now and then tar, pitch, and turpentine were sent from some districts, but the Virginia planter rarely sent anything but tobacco to England in return for what he received.

CHAPTER II.

A VIRGINIA PLANTATION.

LET us visit in imagination one of these Virginia plantations, such as were to be found in 1732, and see what sort of life was led upon it.

To reach the plantation, one is likely to ride for some distance through the woods. The country is not yet cleared of the forest, and each planter, as he adds one tobacco-field to another, has to make inroads upon the great trees. Coming nearer, one rides past tracts where the underbrush is gone, but tall, gaunt trees stand, bearing no foliage and looking ready to fall to the ground. They have been girdled, that is, have had a gash cut around the trunk, through the bark, quite into the wood; thus the sap cannot flow, and the tree rots away, falling finally with a great crash. The luckless traveler sometimes finds his way stopped by one of these trees fallen across the road. By the border of these tracts are Virginia rail-fences, eight or ten feet in height, which zigzag in a curious fashion, — the rails, twelve feet or so in length, not running into posts, but resting on one another at the ends, like a succession of W's. When the new land is wholly cleared of trees, these fences can be removed, stick by stick, and set farther back. No post-holes have to be dug, nor posts driven in.

Now the tobacco-fields come into view. If the plant is growing, one sees long rows of hillocks kept free from weeds, and the plant well bunched at the top, for the lower leaves and suckers are pruned once a week; and as there is a worm which infests the tobacco, and has to be picked off and killed, during the growth of the plant all hands are kept busy in the field.

I have said that there were scarcely any towns or villages in Virginia, so one might fancy there was some mistake; for what means this great collection of houses? Surely here is a village; but look closer. There are no stores or shops or churches or schoolhouses. Rising above the rest is one principal building. It is the planter's own house, which very likely is surrounded by beautiful trees and gardens. At a little distance are the cabins of the negroes, and the gaping wooden tobacco-houses, in which the tobacco is drying, hung upon poles and well sunned and aired, for the houses are built so as to allow plenty of ventilation and sunlight. The cabins of the negroes are low wooden buildings, the chinks filled in with clay. Many of them have kitchen gardens about them, for the slaves are allowed plots of ground on which to raise corn and melons and small vegetables for their own use. The planter's house is sometimes of wood, sometimes of brick, and sometimes of stone. The one feature, however, which always strikes a stranger is the great outside chimney, — usually there is one at each end of the house, — a huge pile of brick or stone, rising above the ridge-pole. Very often, too, there are wide verandas and porches. In this climate, where there are no freezing-cold winters, it is not necessary to build chimneys in the middle of the house, where the warmth of the bricks may serve to temper the air of all the rooms. Moreover, in the warm summers it is well to keep the heat of the cooking away from the house, so the meals are prepared in kitchens built separate from the main house. Inside the great house, one finds one's self in large, airy rooms and halls; wide fireplaces hold blazing fires in the cool days, and in the summer there is a passage of air on all sides. Sometimes the rooms are lathed and plastered, but often they are sheathed in the cedar and other woods which grow abundantly in the country. There is little of that spruce tidiness on which a New England housekeeper prides herself. The house servants are lazy and good-natured, and the people live in a generous fashion, careless of waste, and indifferent to orderly ways.

The planter has no market near by to which he can go for his food; accordingly he has his own smokehouse, in which he cures his ham and smokes his beef; he has outhouses and barns scattered about, where he stores his provisions; and down where the brook runs is the spring-house, built over the running stream. Here the milk and butter and eggs are kept standing in buckets in the cool fresh water. The table is an abundant but coarse one. The woods supply game, and the planter has herds of cattle. But he raises few vegetables and little wheat. The English ship brings him wines and liquors, which are freely used, and now and then one of his negro women has a genius for cooking and can make dainty dishes. The living, however, is rather profuse than nice.

It fits the rude, out-of-door life of the men. The master of the house spends much of his time in the saddle. He prides himself on his horses, and keeps his stables well filled. It is his chief business to look after his estate. He has, to be sure, an overseer, or steward, who takes his orders and sees that the various gangs of negroes do their required work; but the master, if he would succeed, himself must visit the several parts of his plantation and make sure that all goes on smoothly. He must have an eye to his stock, for very likely he has blooded horses; he must see that the tobacco is well harvested; he must ride to the new field which is being cleared, and inspect his fences. There is enough in all this to keep the planter in his saddle all day long.

With horses in the stable and dogs in the kennel, the Virginian is a great hunter. He lives in a country where he can chase not only the fox, but the bear and the wild cat. With other planters he rides after the hounds; and they try their horses on the race-course. The man who can ride the hardest, shoot the surest, lift the heaviest weight, run, leap, and wrestle beyond his fellows, is the most admired.

With so free and independent a life, the Virginian is a generous man, who is hospitable both to his neighbors and to strangers. If he hears of any one traveling through the country and putting up at one of the uncomfortable little inns, he sends for him to come to his house, without waiting for a letter of introduction. He entertains his neighbors, and there are frequent gatherings of old and young for dancing and merry-making. The tobacco crop varies, and the price of it is constantly changing. Thus the planter can never reckon with confidence upon his income, and, with his reckless style of living, he is often in debt. He despises small economies, and looks down upon the merchant and trader, whose business it is to watch closely what they receive and what they pay out.

The Virginian does not often go far from his plantation. His chief journey is to the capital, at Williamsburg, where he goes when the colonial House of Burgesses is in session. Then he gets out his great yellow coach, and his family drive over rough roads and come upon other planters and their families driving through the woods in the same direction. At the capital, during the session, are held balls and other grand entertainments, and the men discuss the affairs of the colony. They honor the king, and pay their taxes without much grumbling, but they are used to managing affairs in Virginia without a great deal of interference from England. The new country helps to make them independent; they are far away from King and Parliament and Court; they are used to rule; and in the defense of their country against Indians and French they have been good soldiers.

But what is the Virginian lady doing all this time? It is not hard to see, when one thinks of the great house, the many servants, the hospitality shown to strangers, and the absence of towns. She is a home-keeping body. She has to provide for her household, and as she cannot go shopping to town, she must keep abundant stores of everything she needs. Often she must teach her children, for very likely there is no school near to which she can send them. She must oversee and train her servants, and set one to spinning, another to mending, and another to sewing; but she does not find it easy to have nice work done; her black slaves are seldom skilled, and she has to send to England for her finer garments. There is no doctor near at hand, and she must try her hand at prescribing for the sick on the plantation, and must nurse white and black.

In truth, the Virginian lady saves the Old Dominion. If it were not for her, the men would be rude and barbarous; but they treat her with unfailing respect, and she gives the gentleness and grace which they would quickly forget. Early in this century some one went to visit an old Virginian lady, and she has left this description of what she saw: —

"On one side sits the chambermaid with her knitting; on the other, a little colored pet learning to sew; an old decent woman is there with her table and shears, cutting out the negroes' winter clothes; while the old lady directs them all, incessantly knitting herself. She points out to me several pair of nice colored stockings and gloves she has just finished, and presents me with a pair half-done, which she begs I will finish and wear for her sake."

CHAPTER III.

THE BOYHOOD OF WASHINGTON.

THE old lady thus described was the widow of George Washington, and so little had life in Virginia then changed from what it had been in 1732, that the description might easily stand for a portrait of George Washington's mother. Of his father he remembered little, for though his mother lived long after he had grown up and was famous, his father died when the boy was eleven years old.

It was near the shore of the Potomac River, between Pope's Creek and Bridge's Creek, that Augustine Washington lived when his son George was born. The land had been in the family ever since Augustine's grandfather, John Washington, had bought it, when he came over from England in 1657. John Washington was a soldier and a public-spirited man, and so the parish in which he lived — for Virginia was divided into parishes as some other colonies into townships — was named Washington. It is a quiet neighborhood; not a sign remains of the old house, and the only mark of the place is a stone slab, broken and overgrown with weeds and brambles, which lies on a bed of bricks taken from the remnants of the old chimney of the house. It bears the inscription : —

Here
The 11th of February, 1732 (old style)
George Wafhington
was born

The English had lately agreed to use the calendar of Pope Gregory, which added eleven days to the reckoning, but people still used the old style as well as the new. By the new style, the birthday was February 22, and that is the day which is now observed. The family into which the child was born consisted of the father and mother, Augustine and Mary Washington, and two boys, Lawrence and Augustine. These were sons of Augustine Washington by a former wife who had died four years before. George Washington was the eldest of the children of Augustine and Mary Washington; he had afterward three brothers and two sisters, but one of the sisters died in infancy.

It was not long after George Washington's birth that the house in which he was born was burned, and as his father was at the time especially interested in some iron-works at a distance, it was determined not to rebuild upon the lonely place. Accordingly Augustine Washington removed his family to a place which he owned in Stafford County, on the banks of the Rappahannock River opposite Fredericksburg. The house is not now standing, but a picture was made of it before it was destroyed. It was, like many Virginia houses of the day, divided into four rooms on a floor, and had great outside chimneys at either end.

Here George Washington spent his childhood. He learned to read, write, and cipher at a small school kept by Hobby, the sexton of the parish church. Among his playmates was Richard Henry Lee, who was afterward a famous Virginian. When the boys grew up, they wrote to each other of grave matters of war and state, but here is the beginning of their correspondence, written when they were nine years old: —

"RICHARD HENRY LEE TO GEORGE WASHINGTON:

"Pa brought me two pretty books full of pictures he got them in Alexandria they have pictures of dogs and cats and tigers and elefants and ever so many pretty things cousin bids me send you one of them it has a picture of an elefant and a little Indian boy on his back like uncle jo's sam pa says if I learn my tasks good he will let uncle jo bring me to see you will you ask your ma to let you come to see me.

"RICHARD HENRY LEE."

"GEORGE WASHINGTON TO RICHARD HENRY LEE:

"DEAR DICKEY I thank you very much for the pretty picture-book you gave me. Sam asked me to show him the pictures and I showed him all the pictures in it; and I read to him how the tame elephant took care of the master's little boy, and put him on his back and would not let anybody touch his master's little son. I can read three or four pages sometimes without missing a word. Ma says I may go to see you, and stay all day with you next week if it be not rainy. She says I may ride my pony Hero if Uncle Ben will go with me and lead Hero. I have a little piece of poetry about the picture book you gave me, but I must n't tell you who wrote the poetry.

> "'G. W.'s compliments to R. H. L.,
> And likes his book full well,
> Henceforth will count him his friend,
> And hopes many happy days he may spend.
> "Your good friend,
> "GEORGE WASHINGTON.

"I am going to get a whip top soon, and you may see it and whip it." [1]

It looks very much as if Richard Henry sent his letter off just as it was written. I suspect that his correspondent's letter was looked over, corrected, and copied before it was sent. Very possibly Augustine Washington was absent at the time on one of his journeys; but at any rate the boy owed most of his training to his mother, for only two years after this his father died, and he was left to his mother's care.

She was a woman born to command, and since she was left alone with a family and an estate to

---

[1] From B. J. Lossing's *The Home of Washington*.

care for, she took the reins into her own hands, and never gave them up to any one else. She used to drive about in an old-fashioned open chaise, visiting the various parts of her farm, just as a planter would do on horseback. The story is told that she had given an agent directions how to do a piece of work, and he had seen fit to do it differently, because he thought his way a better one. He showed her the improvement.

"And pray," said the lady, "who gave you any exercise of judgment in the matter? I command you, sir; there is nothing left for you but to obey."

In those days, more than now, a boy used very formal language when addressing his mother. He might love her warmly, but he was expected to treat her with a great show of respect. When Washington wrote to his mother, even after he was of age, he began his letter, "Honored Madam," and signed it, "Your dutiful son." This was a part of the manners of the time. It was like the stiff dress which men wore when they paid their respects to others; it was put on for the occasion, and one would have been thought very unmannerly who did not make a marked difference between his every-day dress and that which he wore when he went into the presence of his betters. So Washington, when he wrote to his mother, would not be so rude as to say, "Dear Mother."

Such habits as this go deeper than mere forms of speech. I do not suppose that the sons of this lady feared her, but they stood in awe of her, which is quite a different thing.

"We were all as mute as mice, when in her presence," says one of Washington's companions; and common report makes her to have been very much such a woman as her son afterward was a man.

I think that George Washington owed two strong traits to his mother, — a governing spirit and a spirit of order and method. She taught him many lessons and gave him many rules; but, after all, it was her character shaping his which was most powerful. She taught him to be truthful, but her lessons were not half so forcible as her own truthfulness.

There is a story told of George Washington's boyhood — unfortunately there are not many stories — which is to the point. His father had taken a great deal of pride in his blooded horses, and his mother afterward took pains to keep the stock pure. She had several young horses that had not yet been broken, and one of them in particular, a sorrel, was extremely spirited. No one had been able to do anything with it, and it was pronounced thoroughly vicious, as people are apt to pronounce horses which they have not learned to master. George was determined to ride this colt, and told his companions that if they would help him catch it, he would ride and tame it.

Early in the morning they set out for the pasture, where the boys managed to surround the sorrel and then to put a bit into its mouth. Washington sprang upon its back, the boys dropped the bridle, and away flew the angry animal. Its rider at once began to command; the horse resisted, backing about the field, rearing and plunging. The boys became thoroughly alarmed, but Washington kept his seat, never once losing his self-control or his mastery of the colt. The struggle was a sharp one; when suddenly, as if determined to rid itself of its rider, the creature leaped into the air with a tremendous bound. It was its last. The violence burst a blood-vessel, and the noble horse fell dead.

Before the boys could sufficiently recover to consider how they should extricate themselves from the scrape, they were called to breakfast; and the mistress of the house, knowing that they had been in the fields, began to ask after her stock.

"Pray, young gentlemen," said she, "have you seen my blooded colts in your rambles? I hope they are well taken care of. My favorite, I am told, is as large as his sire."

The boys looked at one another, and no one liked to speak. Of course the mother repeated her question.

"The sorrel is dead, madam," said her son. "I killed him!"

And then he told the whole story. They say

that his mother flushed with anger, as her son often used to, and then, like him, controlled herself, and presently said, quietly: —

"It is well; but while I regret the loss of my favorite, I rejoice in my son who always speaks the truth."

The story of Washington's killing the blooded colt is of a piece with other stories less particular, which show that he was a very athletic fellow. Of course, when a boy becomes famous, every one likes to remember the wonderful things he did before he was famous; and Washington's playmates, when they grew up, used to show the spot by the Rappahannock, near Fredericksburg, where he stood and threw a stone to the opposite bank; and at the celebrated Natural Bridge, the arch of which is two hundred feet above the ground, they always tell the visitor that George Washington threw a stone in the air the whole height. He undoubtedly took part in all the sports which were the favorites of his country at that time — he pitched heavy bars, tossed quoits, ran, leaped, and wrestled; for he was a powerful, large-limbed young fellow, and he had a very large and strong hand.

CHAPTER IV.

SCHOOL-DAYS.

THE story of George Washington's struggle with the colt must belong to his older boyhood, when he was at home on a vacation; for we have seen that he had to have his pony led when he was nine years old; and after his father's death, which occurred when he was eleven, he went away to school. When Augustine Washington died, he divided his several estates among his children; but his widow was to have the oversight of the portions left to the younger children until they should come of age. Lawrence Washington received an estate called Hunting Creek, located near a stream of the same name which flowed into the Potomac; and Augustine, his brother, received the old homestead near Bridge's Creek; the mother and younger children continued to live near Fredericksburg.

Both Lawrence and Augustine Washington married soon after their father's death, and as there chanced to be a good school near Bridge's Creek, George Washington now made his home with his brother Augustine, staying with him till he was nearly sixteen years old.

He was to be, like his father, a Virginian planter; and I suppose that had something to do with the kind of training which Mr. Williams, the schoolmaster at Bridge's Creek, gave him. At any rate, it is easy to see what he studied. Most boys' copy-books and exercise-books are early destroyed, but it chances that those of George Washington have been kept, and they are very interesting. The handwriting in them is the first thing to be noticed, — round, fair, and bold, the letters large like the hand that formed them, and the lines running straight and even. In the arithmetics and book-keeping manuals which we study at school, there are printed forms of receipts, bills, and other ordinary business papers: but in Washington's school-days, the teacher probably showed the boys how to draw these up, and gave them, also, copies of longer papers, like leases, deeds, and wills. There were few lawyers in the colony, and every gentleman was expected to know many forms of documents which in these days are left to our lawyers.

Washington's exercise-books have many pages of these forms, written out carefully by the boy. Sometimes he made ornamental letters, such as clerks were wont to use in drawing up such papers. This was not merely exercise in penmanship; it was practice work in all that careful keeping of accounts and those business methods which were sure to be needed by one who had to manage a great plantation. George Washington was to manage something greater, though he did not then know it; and the habits which he formed at this time were of inestimable value to him in his manhood.

The manuscript book which contains these exercises has also a list of a hundred and ten " Rules of Civility and Decent Behavior in Company and Conversation." Probably they were not made up by the boy, but copied from some book or taken down from the lips of his mother or teacher. They sound rather stiff to us, and we should be likely to think the boy a prig who attempted to be governed by them; but it was a common thing in those days to set such rules before children, and George Washington, with his liking for regular, orderly ways — which is evident in his handwriting — probably used the rules and perhaps committed them to memory, to secure an even temper and self-control. Here are a few of them: —

"Every action in company ought to be with some sign of respect to those present.

"When you meet with one of greater quality than yourself, stop and retire, especially if it be at a door or any strait place, to give way for him to pass.

"They that are in dignity or in office have in all places precedency; but whilst they are young, they ought to respect those that are their equals in birth or other qualities, though they have no public charge.

"Strive not with your superiors in argument, but always submit your judgment to others with modesty.

"Be not hasty to believe flying reports to the disparagement of any.

"Take all admonitions thankfully, in what time or place soever given; but afterwards, not being culpable, take a time or place convenient to let him know it that gave them.

"Think before you speak; pronounce not imperfectly, nor bring out your words too hastily, but orderly and distinctly.

"Speak not evil of the absent, for it is unjust.

"Make no show of taking great delight in your victuals; feed not with greediness; cut your bread with a knife; lean not on the table; neither find fault with what you eat.

"Be not angry at table, whatever happens, and if you have reason to be so, show it not; put on a cheerful countenance, especially if there be strangers, for good humor makes one dish of meat a feast.

"Let your recreations be manful, not sinful.

"Labor to keep alive in your breast that little spark of celestial fire called conscience."

These are not unwise rules; they touch on things great and small. The difficulty with most

boys would be to follow a hundred and ten of
them. They serve, however, to show what was
the standard of good manners and morals among
those who had the training of George Washington.
But, after all, the best of rules would have done
little with poor stuff; it was because this boy had
a manly and honorable spirit that he could be
trained in manly and honorable ways. He was a
passionate but not a vicious boy, and so, since his
passion was kept under control, he was all the
stronger for it. The boy that could throw a stone
across the Rappahannock was taught to be gentle,
and not violent; the tamer of the blooded sorrel
colt controlled himself, and that was the reason
he could control his horse.

With all his strength and agility, George
Washington was a generous and fair-minded boy;
otherwise he would not have been chosen, as he
often was, to settle the disputes of his companions.
He was a natural leader. In his boyhood there
was plenty of talk of war. What is known as
King George's War had just broken out between
the English and the French; and there were always
stories of fights with the Indians in the back
settlements. It was natural, therefore, that boys
should play at fighting, and George Washington
had his small military company, which he drilled
and manœuvred.

Besides, his brother Lawrence had been a soldier, and he must have heard many tales of war when he visited him. Thus it came about that he was for throwing his books aside and entering His Majesty's service. He was, however, too young for the army — he was only fifteen; but Lawrence Washington encouraged him, and as he knew many officers in the navy, he had no difficulty in obtaining for his young brother a warrant as midshipman in the navy.

It is said that the young middy's luggage was on board a man-of-war anchored in the Potomac, when Madam Washington, who had all along been reluctant to have her son go to sea, now declared finally that she could not give her consent to the scheme. He was still young and at school; perhaps, also, this Virginian lady, living in a country where the people were not much used to the sea, looked with concern at a profession which would take her oldest boy into all the perils of the ocean. The influence which finally decided her to refuse her consent is said to have been this letter, which she received from her brother, then in England : —

"I understand that you are advised, and have some thoughts of putting your son George to sea. I think he had better be put apprentice to a tinker, for a common sailor before the mast has by no means the common liberty of the subject; for they will press him from a ship where he has fifty shillings a month, and make him take twenty-three, and cut and slash, and use him like a negro, or rather like a dog. And, as to any considerable preferment in the navy, it is not to be expected, as there are always so many gaping for it here who have interest, and he has none. And if he should get to be master of a Virginia ship (which is very difficult to do), a planter that has three or four hundred acres of land, and three or four slaves, if he be industrious, may live more comfortably, and leave his family in better bread, than such a master of a ship can."

It seems possible from this letter that the plan was to put George into the navy that he might come to command a merchant ship; but however that may be, the plan was given up, and the boy went back to school for another year. During that time he applied himself especially to the study of surveying. In a country of great estates, and with a new, almost unexplored territory coming into the hands of planters, surveying was a very important occupation. George Washington, with his love of exactness and regularity, his orderly ways and his liking for outdoor life, was greatly attracted by the art. Five or six years must elapse before he could come into possession of the property which his father had left him; his mother was living on it and managing it. Meanwhile, the work of surveying land would give him plenty of occupation, and bring him in money; so he studied geometry and trigonometry; he made calculations, and he surveyed all the fields about the school-house, plotting them and setting down everything with great exactness.

I wonder if his sudden diligence in study and outdoor work was due at all to an affair which happened about this time. He was a tall, large-limbed, shy boy of fifteen when he fell in love with a girl whom he seems to have met when living with his brother Augustine. He calls her, in one of his letters afterward, a "lowland beauty," and tradition makes her to have been a Miss Grimes, who later married, and was the mother of one of the young soldiers who served under Washington in the War for Independence. Whatever may have been the exact reason that his love affair did not prosper — whether he was too shy to make his mind known, or so silent as not to show himself to advantage, or so discreet with grave demeanor as to hold himself too long in reserve, it is impossible now to say; but I suspect that one effect was to make him work the harder. Sensible people do not expect boys of fifteen to be playing the lover; and George Washington was old for his years, and not likely to appear in the rôle of a spooney.

CHAPTER V.

MOUNT VERNON AND BELVOIR.

ALTHOUGH, after his father's death, George Washington went to live with his brother Augustine for the sake of going to Mr. Williams's school, he was especially under the care of his eldest brother. Lawrence Washington, like other oldest sons of Virginia planters, was sent to England to be educated. After his return to America, there was war between England and Spain, and Admiral Vernon of the English navy captured one of the Spanish towns in the West Indies. The people in the American colonies looked upon the West Indies somewhat differently from the way in which we regard them at present. Not only were the islands on the map of America, but like the colonies, some of them were a part of the British possessions. A brisk trade was kept up between them and the mainland; and indeed, the Bermudas were once within the bounds of Virginia.

So, when Admiral Vernon needed reënforcements, he very naturally looked to the colonies close at hand. A regiment was to be raised and sent out to Jamaica as part of the British forces.

Lawrence Washington, who was a spirited young fellow, obtained a commission as captain in a company of this regiment, and went to the West Indies, where he fought bravely in the engagements which followed. When the war was over he returned to Virginia, so in love with his new profession that he determined to go to England, with the regiment to which his company was attached, and to continue as a soldier in His Majesty's service.

Just then there happened two events which changed his plans and perhaps prevented him from some day fighting against an army commanded by his younger brother. He fell in love with Anne Fairfax, and before they were married his father died. This left his mother alone with the care of a young family, and made him also at once the owner of a larger estate. His father, as I have said, bequeathed to him Hunting Creek, and there, after his marriage, he went to live, as a planter, like his father before him. For the time, at any rate, he laid aside his sword, but he kept up his friendship with officers of the army and the navy; and out of admiration for the admiral under whom he had served, he changed the name of his estate from Hunting Creek to Mount Vernon.

The house which Lawrence Washington built was after the pattern of many Virginian houses of the day, — two stories in height, with a porch running along the front, but with its two chimneys, one at each end, built inside instead of outside. Possibly this was a notion which Lawrence Washington brought with him from England; perhaps he did it to please his English bride. The site which he chose was a pleasant one, upon a swelling ridge, wooded in many places, and high above the Potomac, which swept in great curves above and below, almost as far as the eye could see. Beyond, on the other side, were the Maryland fields and woods.

A few miles below Mount Vernon was another plantation, named Belvoir, and it was here that William Fairfax lived, whose daughter Anne had married Lawrence Washington. Fairfax also had been an officer in the English army, and at one time had been governor of one of the Bahama Islands. Now he had settled in Virginia, where his family had large landed possessions.

He was a man of education and wealth, and he had been accustomed to plenty of society. He had no mind to bury himself in the backwoods of Virginia, and with his grown-up sons and daughters about him, he made his house the centre of gayety. It was more richly furnished than most of the houses of the Virginia planters. The floors were covered with carpets, a great luxury in those days; the rooms were lighted with wax candles; and he had costly wines in his cellars. Servants in livery moved about to wait on the guests, and Virginia gentlemen and ladies flocked to Belvoir.

The master of the house was an officer of the king, for he was collector of customs for the colony and president of the governor's council. British men-of-war sailed up the Potomac and anchored in the stream, and the officers came ashore to be entertained by the Honorable William Fairfax.

The nearness of Mount Vernon and the close connection between the two families led to constant passage between the places. The guests of one were the guests of the other, and George Washington, coming to visit his brother Lawrence, was made at home at Belvoir also. He was a reserved, shy, awkward schoolboy. He was only fifteen when he was thrown into the gay society there, but he was tall, large-limbed, and altogether much older and graver than his years would seem to indicate. He took his place among the men in sports and hunting, and though he was silent and not very lively in his manner, there was something in his serious, strong face which made him a favorite among the ladies.

He met at Belvoir William Fairfax's son, George William, who had recently come home from England, and was just married. He was six years older than George Washington, but that did not prevent them from striking up a warm friendship, which continued through life. The young bride had a sister with her, and this lively girl, Miss Cary, teased and played with the big, overgrown schoolboy. I do not believe he told her what he wrote to one of his boy friends, — that he would have passed his time very pleasantly if all this merriment and young society had not kept him constantly thinking of his "lowland beauty," and wishing himself with her!

But his most notable friend was Thomas, sixth Lord Fairfax, who was at this time staying at Belvoir.[1] He had been a brilliant young man, of university education, an officer in a famous regiment, and at home in the fashionable and literary world of London. But he had suffered two terrible disappointments. His mother and his grandmother, when he was a boy, had so misused the property which descended to him from the Fairfaxes that when he came of age it had been largely lost. Then, later on, just as he was about to be married to a fine lady, she discovered that she could have a duke instead, and so broke the engagement and threw Lord Fairfax aside.

It chanced that his mother had all this while an immense property in Virginia, nearly a fifth of the present State, which the good-natured King Charles the Second had given to her. This was now Lord Fairfax's, and he had appointed his cousin, William Fairfax, his agent to look after it. So, when he found all London pitying him or

[1] He was of the family of the famous Thomas, third Lord Fairfax, who lived in Cromwell's day, and was the head of that house of fighters who took first the side of Parliament and afterward the side of the King.

smiling at him behind his back, he left England to visit his American estate. That had occurred eight years before George Washington's visit to Belvoir. And now Lord Fairfax was back again, for his taste of Virginian life had so charmed him that he had determined to turn his back on London and plunge again into the wilderness of the New World.

He was at this time nearly sixty years of age, gaunt and grizzled in appearance, and eccentric in many of his ways; but people generally laid that to the disappointments which he had met. He was the great man at Belvoir; the younger people looked with admiration upon the fine-mannered gentleman who had been at court, who knew Steele and Addison and other men of letters, and had now come out into the backwoods to live upon his vast estate, the greatest in all Virginia.

His lordship, meanwhile, cared little for the gay society which gathered at Belvoir; he was courtly to the ladies but they saw little of him. He liked best the free, out-of-doors life in the woods and the excitement of the hunt. It was this that had pleased him when he first visited Virginia, and that now had brought him back for the rest of his life. It was not strange, therefore, that a friendship should spring up between him and the tall, grave lad, who was so strong in limb, who sat his horse so firmly and rode after the hounds so well. They hunted together, and the older man came to know familiarly and like the strong young American, George Washington.

What if, in the still night, as they sat over their camp fire, the shy boy had told his gaunt, grizzled friend the secret of the trouble which kept him constrained and silent in the midst of the bright company at Belvoir! I fancy this same friend, schooled in Old World experiences and disappointments, knew how to receive this fresh confidence.

Out of this friendship came a very practical advantage. Neither Lord Fairfax nor his cousin William knew the bounds and extent of the lands beyond the Blue Ridge, which formed an important part of his lordship's domain. Moreover, rumors came that persons from the northward had found out the value of these lands, and that one and another had settled upon them without asking leave or troubling themselves about Lord Fairfax's title. At that time the government had done very little toward surveying the country which lay beyond the borders of population. It was left to any one who claimed such land to find out exactly where it was, and of what it consisted.

Lord Fairfax therefore determined to have his property surveyed, and he gave the commission to his young friend George Washington, who had shown not only that he knew how to do the technical work, but that he had those qualities of courage, endurance, and perseverance which were necessary. The young surveyor had just passed his sixteenth birthday, but, as I have said, he was so serious and self-possessed that his companions did not treat him as a real boy. He did not go alone, for his friend George William Fairfax went with him. As the older of the two, and bearing the name of Fairfax, he was the head of the expedition, but the special work of surveying was to be done by George Washington.

CHAPTER VI.

THE YOUNG SURVEYOR.

IT was in March, 1748, just a month after George Washington was sixteen years old, that the two young men set out on their errand. They were only absent four or five weeks, but it was a sudden and rough initiation into hard life. They were mounted, and crossed the Blue Ridge by Ashby's Gap, entering the Shenandoah Valley and making their first important halt at a spot known as Lord Fairfax's Quarters. The term " quarters " was usually applied at that time to the part of a plantation where the negro slaves lived. Here, in a lonely region near the river, about twelve miles south of the present town of Winchester, Lord Fairfax's overseer had charge of a number of slaves who were cultivating the ground.

The next day after reaching this place, the young surveyor and his companion sent their baggage forward to a Captain Hite's, and followed more slowly, working as they went at their task of laying off land. At the end of a hard day they had supper, and were ready for bed. As young gentlemen, they were shown into a chamber, and

Washington, who had known nothing of frontier life, proceeded as at home. He stripped himself very orderly, he says in the diary which he kept, and went to bed. What was his dismay, instead of finding a comfortable bed like that to which he was used, to discover nothing but a little dirty straw, "without sheet or anything else, but only one threadbare blanket, with double its weight of vermin." He was glad to be out of it, and to dress himself and sleep in his clothes like his companions. After that, he knew better how to manage, and lay wrapped before the fire, especially glad when the fire was out-of-doors and the blue sky overhead formed the counterpane of his bed.

The party followed the Shenandoah to its junction with the Potomac, and then ascended that river and went some seventy miles up the South Branch, returning over the mountains. They were hard at work at the business of surveying, but had plenty of adventure besides. They camped out in the midst of wild storms; they swam their horses over swollen streams; they shot deer and wild turkeys; they visited one of His Majesty's justices of the peace, as Washington takes pains to note. He invited them to supper, but expected them to eat it with their hunting-knives, for he had neither knife nor fork on his table; and when they were near no house they prepared their own suppers, using forked sticks for spits, and chips for plates.

At one place they had the good luck to be on hand when thirty Indians who had been on the war-path came in. "We had some liquor with us," Washington says, " of which we gave them a part. This elevating their spirits, put them in the humor of dancing." So they had a grand war-dance, to the music of a native band which consisted of two pieces, — a pot half full of water, over which a deer-skin was stretched, and a gourd with some shot in it used as a rattle.

This month of roughing it was a novelty to the young Virginian. He was used to living with gentlemen, and he shrank a little from the discomforts which he met. He saw the rude life of the new settlers, and heard them jabbering in the German tongue, which he could not understand. It was a stormy, cold month, one of the hardest of the year in which to lead an outdoor life. Still, he was earning his living, and that made it tolerable. He was paid according to the amount of work he did, and sometimes he was able to earn as much as twenty dollars in a day.

Washington kept a brief diary while he was on the excursion, and very likely he showed it to Lord Fairfax on his return; at any rate, he gave him an account of his adventures, and no doubt expanded the entry at the beginning of the diary, where he writes: "Rode to his Lordship's quarters, about four miles higher up the river Shenandoah. We went through most beautiful groves of sugar-trees, and spent the best part of the day in admiring the trees and the richness of the land." Very likely Lord Fairfax had himself visited his quarters before this, but I think he must have been further stirred by the reports which Washington brought of the country, for not long after he went to live there.

The place known as Lord Fairfax's Quarters, he now called Greenway Court, and he hoped to build a great manor-house in which he should live, after the style of an English earl, surrounded by his tenants and servants. He never built more than a house for his steward, however. It was a long story-and-a-half limestone building, the roof sloping forward so as to form a cover for the veranda, which ran the whole length of the house. The great Virginia outside chimneys were the homes of martins and swallows, and the house itself sheltered the steward and such chance guests as came into the wilderness. Upon the roof were two wooden belfries; the bells were to call the slaves to work, or to sound an alarm in case of an attack by Indians.

Lord Fairfax built for his private lodging a rough cabin only about twelve feet square, a short distance from the larger building. Here he lived the rest of his days. Upon racks on the walls were his guns, and close at hand choice books with which he kept alive his old taste for literature. His hounds walked in and out; and hither, too, came backwoodsmen and Indians. He spent his time hunting and apportioning his great estate amongst the settlers, fixing boundary lines, making out leases, and arranging settlements with his tenants. He gave freely to all who came, but his own life was plain and simple. He kept up, however, in a curious way, his old relation with the fine world of London; for, though he dressed as a hunter, and almost as a backwoodsman, he sent every year to London for new suits of clothes of the most fashionable sort.

I suppose this was in part to enable him to appear in proper dress when he went to his friends' plantations; but perhaps also he wished to remind himself that he was still an English gentleman, and might, whenever he chose, go back to the Old World. But he never did go. He lived to see his young friend become general of the army raised to defend the colonies against the unlawful use of authority by the British crown. Lord Fairfax never believed it unlawful; but he was an old man; he took no part in the struggle, but he lived to hear of the surrender of Cornwallis and the downfall of the British power in the colonies; he received messages of love from the victorious general whom he had first started in the world; and he died soon after — on December 12, 1781 — ninety years old.

It was this commission from Lord Fairfax to survey his lands which made the beginning of

Washington's public life. His satisfactory execution of the task brought him an appointment from the governor as public surveyor. This meant that, when he made surveys, he could record them in the regular office of the county, and they would stand as authority if land were bought and sold. For three years now, he devoted himself to this pursuit, spending all but the winter months, when he could not well carry on field work, in laying out tracts of land up and down the Shenandoah Valley and along the Potomac.

A great deal depended on the accuracy of surveys; for if the surveyor made mistakes, he would be very likely to involve the persons whose land he surveyed in endless quarrels and lawsuits. People soon found out that Washington made no mistakes, and he had his hands full. Years afterward, a lawyer who had a great deal of business with land-titles in the new Virginia country declared that the only surveys on which he could depend were those of Washington.

The young surveyor, by his familiarity with the country, learned where the best lands lay, and he was quick to take advantage of the knowledge, so that many fine sections were taken up by him and others of his family and connections. He saw what splendid prospects the wilderness held out, and by contact with the backwoodsmen and the Indians, he laid the foundation of that broad knowledge of men and woodcraft which stood him in such good stead afterward. He must have seemed almost like one of the Indians themselves, as he stood, grave and silent, watching them around their camp-fires.

His outdoor life, his companionship with rough men, and his daily work of surveying served to toughen him. They made him a self-reliant man beyond his years. People who saw him were struck by the curious likeness which his walk bore to that of the Indians. He was straight as an arrow, and he walked with his feet set straight out, moving them forward with the precision and care which the Indian uses. Especially did his long isolation in the wilderness confirm him in the habit of silence which he had as a boy and kept through life. Living so much by himself, he learned to think for himself and rely on himself.

Meanwhile, though his occupation was thus helping to form his character, he was still learning from his associates. There were three or four houses where he was at home. He went back to his mother at her plantation on the Rappahannock; he was a welcome guest at Belvoir; he visited Lord Fairfax in his cabin, and, as his diary shows, read his lordship's books as well as talked with the quaint old gentleman; and he always had a home with his brother Lawrence at Mount Vernon.

CHAPTER VII.

THE OHIO COMPANY.

WHETHER in the woods or at his friends' houses, George Washington was sure, at this time, to hear much talk of the country which lay to the westward. The English had their colonies along the Atlantic coast, and guarded the front door to the American continent. The French had their military posts along the St. Lawrence and the great lakes, and in the Mississippi and Ohio valleys. They had entered the continent by other doors, and the two nations were like two families living in the same house, each wishing the whole premises and making ready to oust the other.

The French held their possessions in America chiefly by means of forts and trading-posts; the English by means of farms and towns. So, while the French were busy making one fort after another in the interior, meaning to have a line from New Orleans to Quebec, the English were constantly clearing away woods and planting farms farther to the westward and nearer to the French forts. The great Appalachian mountain range kept the two people apart for a time, but English settlers were every year crossing the mountains, and making their way into the fertile valleys beyond.

The Indians who roamed over the country found themselves between two fires. They saw very plainly that if these two foreign nations kept increasing their foothold, there would be little room left for themselves. They saw, too, that the French and the English would not settle down in peace together, nor divide the land between them. Nor were the Indians wholly at peace among themselves. One tribe fought another, and each was very ready to call in the aid of the white man.

So the tribes divided. The French were very willing to have certain Indians on their side, when they should come to blows with the English; the English sought to make friends with other Indians who were the enemies of those that had formed alliance with the French; and a tribe would sometimes change its position, siding now with the French, now with the English.

The region of country which was the prize most eagerly contended for by both nations was that watered by the Ohio River and its tributaries. As yet, there were no white settlements in this region; but both French and English traders made their way into it and carried on a brisk business with the Indians. The two nations now set to work in characteristic fashion to get control of the Ohio Valley. The French began to build forts in commanding positions; the English formed a great land company, the object of which was to send out emigrants from England and the Atlantic colonies to settle in the Ohio Valley, plant farms, and so gain a real possession.

The company thus formed was called the Ohio Company. It was planned in 1748, by Thomas Lee, a Virginian gentleman, who associated with himself thirteen other gentlemen, — one, a London merchant who was to act as the company's agent in England; the others, persons living in Virginia and Maryland. They obtained a charter from the king, and the grant of five hundred thousand acres of land lying chiefly south of the Ohio River and west of the Alleghany Mountains, between the Monongahela and Kanawha rivers. These gentlemen reasoned that the natural passage to the Ohio country lay by the Potomac River and through the breaks in the mountain ranges caused by those branches of the Ohio River which took their rise in Virginia. So they intended that the stream of trade which flowed into the Ohio Valley should take its rise in Maryland and Virginia, and benefit the people of those colonies; and in order to carry out their plans, they proposed to build a road for wagons from the Potomac to the Monongahela.

George Washington's elder brothers Lawrence and Augustine, were both among the original members of the Ohio Company, and when, shortly after its formation, Mr. Lee died, Lawrence Washington became the principal manager. He took a very strong interest in the enterprise, and was particularly desirous of settling a colony of Germans on the company's land. The plans of the Ohio Company were freely discussed at Mount Vernon, and George Washington, who had made himself well acquainted with much of the country which lay on the way to the Ohio, was an interested listener and talker.

There was other talk, however, besides that of trade and settlement. The French were everywhere making preparations to assert their ownership of the western country, and the colonies took the alarm and began also to make ready for possible war. Virginia was divided into military districts, each of which was under the charge of an adjutant-general, whose business it was to attend to the organization and equipment of the militia. George Washington was only nineteen years of age, but his brother Lawrence had such confidence in his ability that he secured for him the appointment of adjutant-general for the military district which included Mount Vernon.

To hold such a post, one must be both a drill-master and something of a tactician, as well as a natural leader and good manager. Washington went to work with a will to qualify himself for his place. His brother had served long enough in the army to be able to give him some help, and Lawrence's comrades in the West Indies campaigns could give even more explicit aid. One of these, Major Muse, was a frequent guest at Mount Vernon, and now undertook to teach George Washington the art of war. He lent the young adjutant military treatises, and drilled him in manual exercises. A Dutch soldier, Jacob Van Braam, who was making a living as fencing-master, gave him lessons in the sword exercise, and Washington had the opportunity afterward of doing his old teacher a good turn by securing him a position in the army of which he was himself an officer.

While he was in the midst of all this military exercise, which was very well suited to the mind of one who had been captain of his school company, he was suddenly obliged to drop his sword and manual, and make ready for a voyage. Lawrence Washington, whose health had been impaired by his campaigning in the West Indies, was ill with consumption; and his physicians ordered him to take a voyage to the West Indies again, — this time to recover, if possible, the health which he had lost there when a soldier. He proposed to pass the winter at Barbadoes, and to take his brother George with him.

The two brothers sailed near the end of September, 1751. George Washington, with his methodical habits, at once began a diary, which he kept on the voyage and during his stay on the island. As two gentlemen from Virginia, they were seized upon at once by the English officers and other residents, and treated with great hospitality. The people who live in a small and isolated settlement like that of Barbadoes are generally very glad to meet some one whom they have not seen every day the year around. So the two brothers dined with this and that new acquaintance, and George, being robust and not needing to spare himself, walked, rode, and drove over the island.

Unfortunately, in the midst of his pleasure, he was seized with small-pox and obliged to keep by himself during the last part of his stay. Vaccination was not understood at that time, and there was nothing to be done, if the small-pox were about, but to have it and have it as lightly as possible. Washington had a strong constitution, and bore this trying illness well, but he carried some slight scars from the disease through the rest of his life.

In his diary he recorded briefly the events of each day of his journey, but at the end of his stay, he filled a few pages with general reflections upon the life on which he had looked, and which was so different from that of Virginia. He was of a frugal mind himself, and was amazed at the shiftless ways of the people of Barbadoes. "How wonderful," he says, "that such people should be in debt, and not be able to indulge themselves in all the luxuries as well as necessaries of life. Yet so it happens. Estates are often alienated for debts. How persons coming to estates of two, three, and four hundred acres (which are the largest) can want, is to me most wonderful."

The exactness which the young surveyor had shown in his plans and in his accounts is very apt to go with great prudence and economy. Up to this time he had had very little money besides what he had earned; but he shows in many ways that he had acquired the fundamental principle of sound living, — never spend money until you have earned it; and to this principle he held all his life. I know that prudence and economy are usually regarded as habits which one acquires by careful training, and so they may be. But with George Washington I suspect these traits were inborn and very nearly allied to genius. He had a genius for order and method; it did not sparkle like a genius for wit or imagination, but one must not think less of it for that reason. Because he was so careful and correct, some people thought him mean and close; but he could afford to be thought so, if his carefulness and correctness kept him scrupulously honest.

After the two brothers had been on the island about six weeks, Lawrence Washington, with the uneasiness of an invalid, was sure that he should be better off in Bermuda, and he resolved to go there as soon as the spring opened. But he longed to see his family, and accordingly sent his brother back to Virginia, intending that he should return later to Bermuda with Mrs. Washington. George had a stormy passage, and reached Virginia in February. There he awaited orders from his brother. But Lawrence Washington, with the caprice and changing mood of a consumptive, could not make up his mind what he most wanted, — whether to send for his wife or to go home himself. At last his disease increased so rapidly as to alarm him, and he hastened home, reaching Mount Vernon only a short time before his death, which took place in July, 1752.

He left a wife and one daughter. It is a sign both of his confidence in his brother George and of his love for him, that he made him, though only twenty years old, one of the executors of his will, and his heir in case his daughter should not live to be of age. As George Washington was more familiar with his brother's affairs than any one else, the other executors left the management of the estate almost entirely to him. From this time, Mount Vernon was his home, — though it must have been a melancholy home at first; for he had looked up to his elder brother since he was a boy, and now it was as if a second father and a dear companion had died.

CHAPTER VIII.

MAJOR WASHINGTON.

For a while George Washington was closely occupied with settling his brother's estate, but he was obliged to busy himself with public affairs also; for there were growing rumors of French movements to the westward, and to these Virginia, as one of the nearest colonies and most concerned, was bound to pay special heed. Robert Dinwiddie, a Scotchman and surveyor of customs in Virginia, had just been appointed lieutenant-governor, which at that time meant resident and acting governor. As a new broom sweeps clean, immediately he was very active. Virginia was divided into four military districts and the militia put into active training. Washington had shown himself so capable before that he was again appointed adjutant-general, with the rank of major; and one of the districts, including the northern counties, was assigned to him.

It was not in the colonies alone that preparations went on. The colonies were a part of the British empire, and a blow struck at them by the French in America was an attack on England by France. England, therefore, sent out cannon and powder to Virginia, and instructed the governor to make all speed and build two forts on the Ohio River, in order to secure the country against French occupation.

But the French had moved before the English. In military affairs, the general who is first on the ground usually has a great advantage; the French were a more military people than the English; the whole occupation by the French in America was an occupation by soldiers; and so, while the English ministry and Governor Dinwiddie and the Virginia militia were making ready to start, the governor of Canada had dispatched troops and supplies into the debatable territory, and was busily engaged in winning over the Indians. Moreover, it was said that he had seized certain English traders and sent them, prisoners, to France.

As soon as the news of this reached Governor Dinwiddie, he determined to send a commissioner to the officer in command of the French forces, and ask by what right Frenchmen were building forts in the king's dominions, and what they were intending to do; why they had made prisoners of peaceable Englishmen; and, as the two nations were not at war, why French soldiers were invading English territory. Moreover, the commissioner was to see the Indian chiefs and make sure that they did not form an alliance with the French.

It was no slight matter for any one to undertake such an errand. He must know something of the country; he must be used to Indians; he must be a person whom the French would respect; above all, he must be strong of body, courageous, prudent, wise, and on the alert; for the journey would be a severe one, and the messenger would need to have what is called a "level head." The king's officers in Virginia would have to act on such information as he brought: how many Frenchmen there were in the Ohio country; how many more were on the way; what they were doing; what were their plans. Of course no one expected that the French commandant would kindly sit down and tell the Virginian commissioner what he meant to do; the commissioner must find that out by his own sagacity.

Now the persons who were most immediately concerned were the members of the Ohio Company. Indeed, it was largely through their agency that the governor of Virginia, who himself was a stockholder, had moved in the matter. Lawrence Washington was dead, but Augustine Washington was interested, and the younger brother, George, had charge of Lawrence Washington's affairs. He knew perfectly what interests were at stake. Besides, he was a backwoodsman; it was no novelty for him to follow trails through the forest; he could deal with Indians; and, above all, he had shown himself a clear-headed, far-sighted young man, whom every one instinctively trusted. He was one of his Majesty's officers, for he was Adjutant-General of the Northern District; and so, though Major George Washington was but twenty-one years old, Governor Dinwiddie and his council selected him for this delicate and weighty mission.

It was no summer jaunt on which he set out. He waited upon the governor at Williamsburg, and was armed with papers duly signed and sealed with the great seal of Virginia, giving him authority as commissioner. On October 30, 1753, he left Williamsburg with a journey of more than a thousand miles before him. He stopped at Fredericksburg to say good-by to his mother, and to engage his old fencing-master, Van Braam, as an interpreter. Washington knew no French, and never learned it. Van Braam pretended to know it well, but really had only an ignorant smattering of the language. Thence he went to Alexandria, where he laid in supplies; and to Winchester, which was the most important frontier settlement, where he provided himself with horses, tents, and other camp equipments.

The real start of the expedition was to be made from Wills Creek, now Cumberland in Maryland, which was the outpost of civilization. Here Washington arrived on November 14, and made up his little company. It consisted of Christopher Gist, who was in the employ of the Ohio

Company, and was an experienced frontiersman; of Jacob Van Braam, the French interpreter; of Davidson, an Indian interpreter; and of four frontiersmen. The party was now complete, and the next day they plunged into the wilderness.

Gist knew the way as far as an Indian village called Logstown, on the banks of the Ohio, about seventeen miles from where Pittsburg now stands; there they were to call together the Indian chiefs and confer with them. It had been raining and snowing so heavily in the mountains that they were a week making their way to the Monongahela River at Turtle Creek. Here they found the river so swollen that they saw it was impossible to cross with their pack-horses. Accordingly, they sent all their baggage down the river in a canoe, under charge of two of the men, while the rest swam their horses across and rode down to the rendezvous at the fork of the Ohio, ten miles below.

The Ohio Company had proposed to build a fort about ten miles away from the junction of the Monongahela and Alleghany; here lived a friendly Indian, Shingiss, and that may have determined their plans. But Washington, who reached the fork of the rivers before the canoe, began at once to look over the ground, and decided without hesitation that the real site for the fort should be the point of land which lay between the two rivers.

Shingiss went on with the party to Logstown,

and there Washington stayed five days, conferring with the Indian chiefs and gathering information from some French deserters who happened to be there. He was impatient to go forward to the French forts, but he knew something of Indian ways, and he was learning more. The chiefs sat and talked and smoked, and were silent, and shook their heads, and said it was a serious matter. Serious, indeed, it was to the poor Indians, for the French had already told them that they were coming in force in the spring to drive the English out of the country; but if the English proved too strong for that, then French and English would agree and divide the land between them. As in that case the Indians would have small favor, the French advised the chiefs to side with them against the English.

At last Washington persuaded the Indians to let three of their chiefs and an old hunter accompany his party to where the French were, and they followed the Alleghany to Venango, now Franklin in Venango County, Pennsylvania, where were a few Frenchmen who had driven out an English trader. But the really important station was Fort le Bœuf.

The Frenchmen tried to entice the Indians from Washington, and otherwise to keep him from going on; but he insisted on carrying out his plans, and toiled for four more days through mire and snow-drifts until he came to the fort.

The French commandant, M. de Saint Pierre, received the Virginian commissioner politely, and entertained him for a few days with hospitality, but in the mean time did his utmost to win from Washington the Indian chiefs who had accompanied him. Finally, however, M. de Saint Pierre drew up a formal reply to Governor Dinwiddie's letter, and Washington and his party returned by canoe to Venango, having sent the horses and baggage on in advance.

Now began a terrible journey. The horses were so weak, but so necessary for carrying the baggage, that Washington and his companions set out on foot, while the horses followed behind. Washington was dressed as an Indian, and for three days they kept on in this way, the horses losing strength, the cold increasing, and the roads growing worse. Then Washington, seeing how slowly the party was moving, determined to take Gist with him, and push through the woods, the nearest way, leaving the rest of the company together with the horses and baggage under charge of Van Braam to follow as well as they could.

It was the day after Christmas when he started. He put his journal and other papers into a pack which he strapped to his back, wrapped himself in a stout coat, took his gun in his hand, and set off alone with Gist. They were only a few miles from Venango, and they meant to follow the path a short distance to an Indian village called Murdering Town, and then go by the compass through the woods in as straight a line as possible to the fork of the Ohio. The village was well-named; for shortly after they had left it, they were fired at by a French Indian whom they had taken along there as a guide. They pretended to think that his gun went off for some other reason; but they kept him with them, watching him very closely all day till nine o'clock that night. Then they sent him home. But they knew well that he would rally his friends and pursue them; so they walked all that night and the next day, reaching the Ohio River at dark, and rested there over night.

They supposed, of course, that they should find the river frozen tight and could cross on the ice, but to their dismay, it was frozen only near the shore, while blocks of ice were swirling down the middle of the stream. "There was no way of getting over," says Washington in his journal, "but on a raft, which we set about, with but one poor hatchet, and finished just after sun-setting. This was a whole day's work; we next got it launched, then went on board of it, and set off; but before we were half-way over, we were jammed in the ice in such a manner that we expected every moment our raft to sink and ourselves to perish. I put out my setting-pole to try to stop the raft, that the ice might pass by, when the rapidity of the stream threw it with so much violence against the pole that it jerked me out into ten feet water; but I fortunately saved myself by catching hold of one of the raft-logs. Notwithstanding all our efforts, we could not get to either shore, but were obliged, as we were near an island, to quit our raft and make to it. The cold was so extremely severe that Mr. Gist had all his fingers and some of his toes frozen, and the water was shut up so hard that we found no difficulty in getting off the island on the ice in the morning, and went to Mr. Frazier's."

Here they succeeded in getting horses, and in a few days Washington was at Williamsburg and reporting to the governor. He had not merely made a very difficult journey in the depth of winter and brought back an answer to the governor's letter; but he had made the most minute observations of the condition and plans of the French; he had also strengthened the friendship of the English and Indians; and by patient, unwearied, and resolute attention to the object of his mission, he had brought back a fund of extremely valuable information for the use of the colony. There could be no doubt in the minds of his friends, after reading his journal, that here was a man who could be depended upon. They had known him as a prudent, careful, economical, deliberate, rather silent young fellow, whose judgment was worth having; but I doubt if they had fully perceived before what indomitable courage he had, how fearless he was in the midst of danger, how keen and wary in his dealing with an enemy, and how full of resources and pluck when difficulties arose. Here was no sunshine soldier.

CHAPTER IX.

FORT DUQUESNE AND FORT NECESSITY.

THE House of Burgesses was not in session when Washington made his report to Governor Dinwiddie. But no time was to be lost, and the energetic governor and council issued orders to erect a fort at once upon the point of land at the fork of the Ohio, which Washington had recommended as the best site. Washington was to have command of the two companies of men who were to be enlisted for this purpose, but he was to remain for the present at Alexandria, organizing the expedition, while his second in command, Captain Trent, a trader and frontiersman, went forward with such men as he could raise in the back settlements, and began the construction of the fort.

Lord Fairfax took a lively interest in his young friend's business, but it was not so easy to enlist men for an expedition of this kind, as it was to raise and drill a company of militia, which, by the laws of the colony, could not be marched more than five miles from the boundary line of the colony. Throughout the winter months Washington was hard at work raising his company and putting them in readiness. He had a sorry lot of volunteers to work with; they were for the most part shiftless fellows who had nothing else to do, and scarcely anything to their backs. They were good-natured, however, and ready to buy clothing if the major would pay them their wages; but the major had no money of his own to advance, and he had hard work getting any from the government. He had to reason with his men, humor them, and fit them for service as well as he could. It was capital preparation for a kind of work which he had to do on a large scale afterward.

The governor, meanwhile, had been stirring up the governors of the other colonies, and had called the burgesses together. He could not make every one feel his own need of action; but he persuaded the burgesses to vote a sum of money, and thus was able to enlarge the military force to six companies. There was a proposition to put Washington in command of the entire force; but the young major was reluctant to assume such a charge, when he had had so little experience in handling troops. "I have too sincere a love for my country," he said, "to undertake that which may tend to the prejudice of it."

Accordingly Joshua Fry, an English gentleman of education, was commissioned as colonel, and Washington was given the second place, with rank of lieutenant-colonel. Fry now remained at Alexandria and Washington pushed forward to Wills

Creek, with about a hundred and fifty men, intending to join Trent and complete the fort which he had begun. He reached Wills Creek with his ragged, half-drilled men on April 20, and soon received a very disagreeable piece of news.

Trent, for some reason, had left the fort which he was building, and his second in command having also absented himself, the next highest officer, Ensign Ward, was left in command of the company, which numbered forty-one men. Suddenly there had appeared a multitude of canoes and other craft coming down the Alleghany. It was a large French force dispatched by the governor of Canada to occupy the same point of land. Ward, of course, could do nothing. He was permitted to withdraw with his men, and the French at once pulled down the fort which Trent had begun, and set to work building another and larger one which they named Fort Duquesne. Here, after the wars of the next thirty years were over, the city of Pittsburgh began to rise.

The taking of the post by an armed force was like a declaration of war on the part of France. It was the beginning of the great seven years' war between France and England which ended in the fall of France in America, and led by swift steps to the independence of the colonies. By a strange coincidence, the nearest English force was under the command of a young Virginian officer of militia, only twenty-two years old, who was afterward to be the leader of the colonies in their war against England, and to have the aid of the very France which he was now fighting.

Washington did not hesitate. He at once sent a messenger with the news to Governor Dinwiddie, and wrote letters to the governors of Maryland and Pennsylvania, urging them to send forward troops; for each colony acted independently of the others. Then he began work with such men and materials as he had, meaning to push through the woods to where Red Stone Creek empties into the Monongahela, about half-way to Fort Duquesne, and to build a fort there. It was a spot where Gist had already constructed a storehouse for the Ohio Company. By this plan, Washington would be keeping his men at work, and would have a road built for the use of the troops yet to come. At that point, moreover, there was water communication with Fort Duquesne.

Washington built his road and marched his men until he reached a level piece of grassland, partially covered with bushes, that lay at the foot of Laurel Hill, a spur of the Alleghanies, and was called Great Meadows. It was a good place for a camp, and a good place for fighting if he should be attacked. His scouts had been out, and his Indian friends were on the watch for him. Word came that a French party had left Fort Duquesne and were intending to engage with the first English forces they should meet, for they had heard that the English were on the move.

Washington at once made ready for the attack. There was a gully crossing the field, which he turned into an intrenchment. He also cut down the bushes; but he did not wait for the enemy. He feared they might surprise his camp; and getting word from the Indians that they had discovered, as they thought, the place where the French were hidden, he took forty men, and at ten o'clock at night, in the midst of a hard rain, set out to surprise the enemy.

"The path," he says, " was hardly wide enough for one man; we often lost it, and could not find it again for fifteen or twenty minutes, and we often tumbled over each other in the dark."

At sunrise, May 28, 1754, Washington reached the camp where his Indian friends were. They joined him, and the impetuous young soldier led his combined forces, Indian file, in a stealthy march through the woods to the rocky hollow where the Frenchmen lay concealed. As soon as the English came upon them, the Frenchmen sprang up and raised their guns. Washington, who was in front, gave his men the order to fire, and a sharp engagement followed. Ensign Jumonville, commanding the French party, and nine others were killed. On the English side, one man was killed and two or three wounded. Twenty-two prisoners were taken, and Washington marched back with them to the camp at Great Meadows.

It turned out that Jumonville and his men were an advance party sent out from Fort Duquesne to reconnoitre. They had discovered Washington's force, and being fewer in number, had sent back to the fort for reënforcements. Meanwhile, they were in hiding when surprised by Washington, and had no chance to escape. The young Virginian lieutenant-colonel had every reason to believe that his force was to be attacked, and he acted promptly. He did not stop to parley with them, but answered their raised guns with an order to his men to fire.

The first shot had been fired, and Washington was the man who had fired it. He knew well what would be the immediate consequence of his act; the French would come in force as soon as they heard the news, and he began at once to prepare for defense. He threw up earthworks and made a palisade, and named it Fort Necessity. It was a slight enough protection. He sent his prisoners to Winchester, and informed Governor Dinwiddie of what he had done. "Your Honor may depend," he says, "I will not be surprised, let them come at what hour they will; and this is as much as I can promise. But my best endeavors shall not be wanting to effect more. I doubt not if you hear I am beaten, but you will hear at the same time that we have done our duty, in fighting as long as there was a shadow of hope."

The camp was now a lively place. The Indians,

afraid of the French, began to flock to it, and the companies left behind at Wills Creek now came up; but Colonel Fry was dead, and Washington was in sole command, after all. Meanwhile, Captain Mackay came with a company from South Carolina. He was a captain of the regular army, and so could not serve under a colonial officer; but he was a man of sense and courtesy, and, by mutual consideration, he and Washington avoided any serious conflict of authority. But the volunteer and regular troops could not agree so well; the camp was becoming crowded, and Washington, anxious to carry out his plans, left Captain Mackay in command at Great Meadows, and moved his men thirteen miles further, to a place where Gist had formed a small settlement. It took two weeks to do this, for the men built a road as they went, and the way led through a mountain gorge.

Of course this forward movement was made known to the French by their scouts, and Washington had his scouts out quite as far as Fort Duquesne itself. Soon reports came thick and fast that the French post had been strongly reenforced, and that a large body of men was preparing to descend upon the English. Washington sent for Captain Mackay and his company, and they arrived near the end of June. A council of war was held, and the situation studied. The place where they were was unsuited for defense, since hills surrounded it. The enemy's force was much greater than their own, and they were in no condition to make a successful resistance.

The order to retreat was given. Washington, who had the courage to lead an attack, had also the patience, the self-control, and the cheerful spirit which are so necessary in a retreat. The horses were broken down and the men had to drag the heavy guns themselves. Washington loaded his own horse with public stores and went afoot. He would not even require the soldiers to carry his own baggage, as he might have done, but paid them for the labor. So, on July 2, they were back at Great Meadows. They did not mean to stay there, for though it was a good field for an open fight, it had no natural protection, and Fort Necessity was a hasty, flimsy affair. But the men were exhausted; they had been without sufficient provision for some time, and they were expecting supplies from below.

They strengthened the fort as well as they could, but the French were only a few hours behind them. The very next morning they came in sight, nine hundred strong, not counting Indians. Now was the time for boldness; it was too late to retreat. Washington led his little army out before the fort as if to invite attack; if the Frenchmen came on, he might, in a fair fight, beat them; but they did not come on. They remained at the border of the woods in a position where they could cut off his retreat, and began firing from a distance. Washington, accordingly, withdrew his men behind the embankment.

For nine hours the two forces faced each other, sending shots through the heavy rain and the mist which almost shut them out from each other's sight. There had been a heavy loss on both sides, but when night fell the English were in a desperate condition, half starved, their powder nearly gone, and their guns almost good for nothing. The French proposed a parley. Washington refused, thinking they meant to send an officer who would find out in what a deplorable condition they were. But when they proposed that he should send an officer to them, he consented, and sent Jacob Van Braam, who was now a captain, and the only uninjured officer who understood French.

Van Braam came back, bringing with him in writing the terms upon which the French would accept a surrender. The terms were on the whole liberal. The English were to carry with them everything in their possession except their artillery, were to promise to build no more forts there or beyond the mountains for a year, and were to return the prisoners taken when Jumonville was killed. As a security for this last, two officers were to be left with the French as hostages. Washington accepted the terms, and the next morning began his march back to Wills Creek. From there he and Captain Mackay went to Williamsburg to report in person to the governor.

Failure is sometimes quite as necessary to character as success. It must have been with a heavy heart that the young colonel turned back from Fort Necessity that 4th of July, 1754, his expedition broken up, his military ardor damped, his eye resting on the miserable men whom he was leading away from the bloody field of Great Meadows. He was only twenty-two years old. Twenty-one years after the day when he marshaled his men before Fort Necessity, he was to draw his sword at the head of an American army.

CHAPTER X.

A TERRIBLE LESSON IN WAR.

However keenly Washington may have felt the defeat which he suffered at Great Meadows, no one blamed him for a misfortune which he had tried in so spirited a fashion to prevent. On the contrary, the House of Burgesses, then in session, after hearing an account of the engagement and reading the articles of capitulation, passed a vote of thanks to Colonel Washington and his officers, "for their bravery and gallant defense of their country." In point of fact, the expedition had by no means been a failure. It had built many miles of road; it had shown that the Virginian soldiers could fight, and it had made the French respect their enemy.

To Washington it had been an initiation into military service. He had heard the bullets whistling about him, and had known what it was to lead men; he had encountered on a small scale the difficulties which beset commanders of armies; he had stood for nine hours under fire from a superior force. Not all the hardships of the sharp campaign could dampen his ardor. He knew that he was a soldier; he knew, too, that he was a commander, and such knowledge is much more than petty conceit.

He was to be put to the test in this matter in a new way. He went back to Alexandria, where his regiment was quartered, and shortly after received word from Governor Dinwiddie to be in readiness for a fresh movement. It had been resolved to send another expedition to attack Fort Duquesne, and Washington was bidden at once to fill up his regiment to three hundred men and join the other forces at Wills Creek. Eager as the young colonel was for service, he had not taken leave of his good sense. He was something more than a fighter, and his native judgment, as well as his hard-earned experience, showed him the foolhardiness of such an adventure. It does not appear that he wrote to his superior officer, the governor, remonstrating against the wild project, but he wrote to Lord Fairfax, who had influence, giving his reasons why the enterprise was morally impossible.

They were without men, money, or provisions. It would be impossible in any case to move before November, and he knew well enough, by his experience the year before, what a terrible winter campaign it would be. "To show you the state of the regiment," he writes to Lord Fairfax, "I have sent you a report by which you will perceive what great deficiencies there are of men, arms, tents, kettles, screws (which was a fatal want before), bayonets, cartouch-boxes, and everything else. Again, were our men ever so willing to go, for want of the proper necessaries of life they are unable to do it. The chief part are almost naked, and scarcely a man has either shoes, stockings, or a hat. These things the merchants will not credit them for. The country has made no provision; they have not money themselves, and it cannot be expected that the officers will engage for them again, personally, having suffered greatly on this head already; especially now, when we have all the reason in the world to believe that they will desert whenever they have an opportunity. There is not a man that has a blanket to secure him from cold or wet. Ammunition is a material object, and that is to come from Williamsburg or wherever the governor can procure it. An account must be first sent of the quantity which is wanted; this, added to the carriage up, with the necessary tools that must be had, as well as the time for bringing them round, will, I believe, advance us into that season, when it is usual, in more moderate climates, to retreat into winter-quarters, but here, with us, to begin a campaign!"

The argument of Washington's letter, of which this is a part, was unanswerable. It showed his clear, cool judgment, and the thoroughness with which he considered every detail in a scheme. The governor gave up his design, but it was not long before he stumbled into a new folly. He had persuaded the burgesses to grant twenty thousand pounds for military operations, and had received ten thousand more from England. So he set about enlarging the army to ten independent companies of one hundred men each, proposing to place each company under command of a captain. He hoped in this way to be rid of the jealousy which existed between the several officers, since there would be none above the rank of captain.

The plan was only inferior to one by which every soldier who enlisted should have been made captain, so that nobody need be inferior to anybody else. Washington not only saw the folly of the proceeding from a military point of view (for many of his difficulties had arisen from the presence of independent companies in the field with his troops), but he resented the plan as at once reducing him from the rank of colonel to that of captain. He had risen to the position which he held by regular promotion for bravery and soldierly qualities. He could not be' the football of a capricious governor, and he resigned his commission.

He was instantly wanted in another quarter. Governor Sharpe of Maryland had received a commission from the king, as commander-in-chief of all the forces in America engaged against the French. As soon as it was known that Washington had resigned his commission as colonel of a Virginia regiment, Governor Sharpe sent to invite him to return to the service under his command. He was to have command of a company, but to retain his rank as colonel. Washington replied at once that he could not think of accepting service upon such terms. He was not to be cajoled into assuming a false position. He cared little for the title. What he wanted was the authority which goes with the title. There was no pressing danger to the country, and he was not so impatient to be in military service that he needed as a soldier to throw away the position which he had fairly won.

There was one consideration which especially determined Washington against serving either as captain of an independent company in Virginia, or as one of Governor Sharpe's captains, with the complimentary title of colonel. By a regulation of government, all officers commissioned by the king took rank above officers commissioned by the governors of provinces. It seems that the English authorities were determined to make the colonies understand that their militia officers were always inferior to the regular army officers who came over from England.

There was such an officer sent over shortly after this to take command of all the forces in the colonies. This was Major-General Edward Braddock. He had been in military service forty-five years, and he knew all the rules of war. He was a brave, hot-headed man, who knew to a nicety just how troops should be drawn up, how they should march and perform all the evolutions, how a captain should salute his superior officer, and how much pipeclay a soldier needed to keep his accoutrements bright. He was a rigid disciplinarian, and was called harsh and cruel, but that, very likely, was because he demanded strict and instant obedience.

In February, 1755, General Braddock arrived in Virginia, with his two regiments of regular troops from England. Governor Dinwiddie was delighted. He should have no more trouble with obstinate burgesses and quarrelsome Virginia captains. Everybody expected that the French would at once be driven out of the Ohio Valley, and General Braddock was not the least confident. There was a bustle in every quarter, and Alexandria was made the headquarters from which troops, military stores, and provisions were to be sent forward, for they could be brought up the river to that point in men-of-war and transports.

As soon as Braddock had arrived in the country, Washington had addressed him a letter of welcome, and now he was keenly intent on the general's movements. From Mount Vernon he could see the ships in the Potomac and hear the din of preparation. He could not ride into town or to Belvoir without being in the midst of the excitement. This was something very different from the poor, niggardly conduct of war which he had known in the colony. It was on a great scale; it was war carried on by his Majesty's troops, well-clad, splendidly equipped, and drilled under the lead of a veteran general. He longed to join them. Here would be a chance such as he had never had, to learn something of the art of war; but he held no commission now, and had not even a company to offer. Nor was he willing to be a militia captain and subject to the orders of some lieutenant in the regular army.

He was considering how he might volunteer, when he received exactly the kind of invitation which he desired. He was a marked man now, and it did not take long for word to reach General Braddock that the young Virginian colonel, who had shown great spirit and ability in the recent expedition, and was thoroughly familiar with the route they were to take, desired to serve under him, but not as a subordinate captain. There was a way out of the difficulty, and the general at once invited Washington to join his military family as aid-de-camp.

Washington joyfully accepted. There was only one drawback to his pleasure. His mother, as soon as she heard of his decision, was filled with alarm, and hurried to Mount Vernon to beg her son to reconsider. No doubt they both remembered how, at her earnest wish, he had abandoned his purpose to join the British navy, eight or nine years before. But these eight or nine years had made a great difference. He was a man now, and, without loss of respect for his mother, he was bound to decide for himself. He would be a loser by the step in many ways. There was no one to whom he could intrust the management of his affairs at Mount Vernon, and his attendance on General Braddock would involve him in considerable expense. Nor could he expect, as a mere aid-de-camp, to advance his interests in the military profession. Nevertheless, Washington had counted the cost, and not even his mother's entreaties turned him from his purpose.

At Alexandria, Washington first saw Braddock; he met there also the governors of Virginia, Maryland, Pennsylvania, New York, and Massachusetts, who gathered for a grand council on the campaign. Washington, quiet but observant, looked upon all the preparations with admiration, but without losing his coolness of judgment. He saw the heavy artillery which Braddock had brought, and which was waiting for teams to transport it over the mountains. He remembered how his men had toiled in dragging their few guns over the rough road. "If our march is to be regulated by the slow movements of the train," he said, "it will be tedious, very tedious indeed."

Early in May, Washington joined General Braddock at Fredericktown, Maryland, and there he must have met a man of more consequence than all the governors of the colonies; for Benjamin

Franklin, Postmaster-General of Pennsylvania, at that time a man of fifty years, came to confer with General Braddock, and to do for him what no one else could — procure horses and wagons enough to transport his supplies and artillery. Franklin and Washington probably seemed to most people at that time as rather insignificant persons beside the Major-General in command of the English forces in America.

The headquarters were moved to Wills Creek, where the militia had been hard at work with axe and spade, and had built a fort which was named Fort Cumberland, from the Duke of Cumberland, Captain-General of the British army. For a month Braddock fretted and fumed over the delays which everybody seemed to cause. He was thoroughly out of patience with all his surroundings. There were in all about twenty-two hundred men gathered in camp. Some of these were Virginia troops, and Braddock set his officers to drilling them, but he thought them a slouchy lot that never could be made into soldiers. Indeed, it would have taken a long time to make them into such machines as the soldiers whom he had brought over from England. Washington was fast learning many things. He was not deceived by appearances. He found this great general an obstinate, hot-tempered man, who would scarcely listen to reason, and his soldiers, with all their military training, of different stuff from the Virginians.

BRADDOCK'S HEADQUARTERS AT FREDERICK-TOWN.
From a photograph taken during the War for the Union.

Washington was sent off on an errand to Williamsburg for money. He performed his duty with great promptness, and a week after his return to camp, the army was on the move. But it moved like a snail, for it was carrying a whole house on its back. Braddock and his officers, accustomed to campaigns in Europe, seemed to be unable to adapt themselves to the different conditions of a new country. They encumbered themselves with everything which English army regulations permitted. Washington saw the folly of the course pursued, and, when his advice was asked by the general, urged him, he says, in the warmest terms he was able to use, "to push forward, if even with a small but chosen band, with such artillery and light stores as were necessary, leaving the heavy artillery, baggage, and the like, with the rear division of the army, to follow by slow and easy marches, which they might do safely, while we were advanced in front;" and in order to enforce his opinion and to lead the officers to give up some of their superfluous baggage, and thus release horses for more necessary work, he gave up his own best horse, and took no more baggage than half his portmanteau could easily contain.

His advice prevailed, and he set out with the advance party. It was a prospect, he wrote to his brother, which conveyed infinite delight to his mind, though he was excessively ill at the time.

"But this prospect was soon clouded, and my hopes brought very low indeed, when I found that, instead of pushing on with vigor, without regarding a little rough road, they were halting to level every molehill, and to erect bridges over every brook, by which means we were four days in getting twelve miles." Ill, indeed, he was, and for a fortnight so prostrated with fever that he was forced to lie in hospital. But as soon as he could move at all, he insisted on rejoining his corps. "My fevers are very moderate," he writes to one of the other aids on the last day of June, "and I hope, near terminating. Then I shall have nothing to encounter but weakness, which is excessive, and the difficulty of getting to you, arising therefrom; but this I would not miss doing, before you reach Duquesne, for five hundred pounds. However, I have no doubt now of doing it, as I am moving on, and the general has given me his word of honor, in the most solemn manner, that it shall be effected."

On July 8, he succeeded in rejoining the advance division of the army, though he had to be carried in a covered wagon. On July 9, he attended the general on horseback, though he was still very ill and weak. He had joined Braddock's military family because he wished to learn how an experienced English general practiced the art of war, and how regularly trained troops fought. He was to have the opportunity that day. They had reached a ford on the Monongahela, fifteen miles from Fort Duquesne, and had crossed it. A second ford lay five miles below, and the troops marched, as if on dress parade, down the bank of the river. Braddock intended that the French, if they saw him, should be dismayed by the array, and Washington was often heard to say, in after years, that the most beautiful spectacle he had ever beheld was the display of the British troops on that eventful morning. Every man was neatly dressed in full uniform, the soldiers were arranged in columns and marched in exact order, the sun gleamed from their burnished arms; the river flowed tranquilly on their right, and the deep forest overshadowed them with solemn grandeur on their left. Officers and men were equally inspirited with cheering hopes and confident anticipations.

But Washington was not so dazzled by this brilliant spectacle as not to see the fatal blunder which Braddock was making. He urged the general to throw out Virginia rangers and Indian scouts into the woods and ravines which lay before them and on their side. It is almost incredible that the general paid no attention to the caution, and merely kept a few skirmishers a short way in advance of his force. His army was now across the second ford and moving along the other bank, eight miles only from the fort. Suddenly a man dressed like an Indian, but bearing the decoration of an officer, sprang forward from the woods, faced the column a moment, then turned and waved his hat.

It was an officer leading the French forces, which, accompanied by a horde of Indian allies, had issued from Fort Duquèsne and had disposed themselves in the wood. Another instant, and a storm of bullets rained down upon the Englishmen. It was a surprise, but the troops were well trained. They fired volley after volley into the wood. They planted their cannon and went to work in a business-like way, cheering as they moved forward. For a moment the French seemed to give way; then, in another instant, again the bullets fell from all sides upon the Englishmen, who were bewildered by the attack. They could scarcely see any man; there was nothing to aim at. The enemy was indeed invisible, for every man had posted himself, Indian fashion, behind a tree. Now the troops huddled together into a solid square and made so much the more deadly mark for the rifles. They fell into a panic; they began to leave their guns and to retreat.

Braddock, who had been in the rear, came up with the main body and met the vanguard on its retreat. The two columns of men were thrown into confusion. The Virginians alone, whom Braddock had so despised for their negligent bearing, kept their heads, and promptly adopting tactics familiar to them, screened themselves, as did the enemy, behind trees. But Braddock, to whom such methods were contrary to all the rules of war, ordered them, with oaths, to form in line. The general was a brave man, and if personal courage could have saved the day, his intrepidity would have done it. He dashed about on horseback. Two of his aids were wounded, and the duty of carrying the general's orders fell on the third, Colonel Washington, who was now learning war with a vengeance. He rode in every direction, his tall, commanding figure a conspicuous mark for the enemy's sharpshooters. More than that, there were men there who had met him at Great Meadows, and who now made him their special mark. He had four bullets through his coat, and two horses shot under him. He seemed to escape injury as by a miracle.

Braddock at last ordered a retreat, and while he and such of his officers as remained were endeavoring to bring the panic-stricken troops into some kind of order, he was mortally wounded and fell from his horse. He was borne on a litter, but laid at last at the foot of a tree near the scene of Washington's fight at Fort Necessity, where he died in the night of July 13. The chaplain was wounded, and Washington read the burial service over the body of the general. It was a sorry ending of the expedition which had set out with such high hopes.

Five days later Washington reached Fort Cumberland, and one of his first duties was to send a letter to his mother. "I am still in a weak and feeble condition," he writes, "which induces me to halt here two or three days in the hope of recovering a little strength, to enable me to proceed homewards, from whence, I fear, I shall not be able to stir till towards September; so that I shall not have the pleasure of seeing you till then, unless it be in Fairfax."

He arrived at Mount Vernon on July 26.

CHAPTER XI.

COMMANDER-IN-CHIEF OF THE VIRGINIA FORCES.

THE disastrous defeat of Braddock filled the Virginia people with uneasiness, for it was sure to be followed by Indian raids. The House of Burgesses voted a sum of money, and resolved to increase the regiment by making it consist of sixteen companies. His friends immediately began to urge Washington to solicit the command, but he would do nothing of the sort. His experience had taught him the weakness of the colonial military system; if he were to seek the place he could not at the same time propose reforms. If the command were offered him, that would be a different matter, for then he would be at liberty to make conditions.

The command was offered to him on his own terms, and for three years he was engaged in as trying and perplexing a business as could well be committed to a young man of twenty-three to twenty-six years of age. He did not know it at the time, but we see now that he was attending a school of the severest sort in preparation for the arduous task which was to be set him later in life.

His headquarters were at Winchester, where he

had the active support of his old friend Lord Fairfax. As soon as he had effected some sort of organization, he sent out recruiting officers and did his best to fill up the ranks of his little army. Then he was off on a tour of inspection, visiting the outposts and making himself acquainted, by personal observation, with all the details of his command.

Everything seemed to be against him, and every advantage which he gained was won only by the most determined effort. He must often have thought with envy of the profusion of military stores of all kinds with which Braddock's army was provided, and of the abundant money in the hands of the paymaster. Here was he, obliged to use the strictest economy if he would make the money which the burgesses doled out answer the needs of his command, and he was forced to be his own commissary and quartermaster, laying in stores and buying cattle up and down the country. "At the repeated instance of the soldiers," he writes once to the Speaker of the House, "I must pay so much regard to their representations, as to transmit their complaints. They think it extremely hard, as it is indeed, sir, that they, who perhaps do more duty, and undergo more fatigue and hardship from the nature of the service and situation of the country, should be allowed the least pay, and smallest encouragements in other respects. Our soldiers complain that their pay is insufficient even to furnish shoes, shirts, and stockings, which their officers, in order to keep them fit for duty, oblige them to provide. This, they say, deprives them of the means of purchasing any of the conveniences or accessories of life, and compels them to drag through a disagreeable service, in the most disagreeable manner. That their pay will not afford more than enough to keep them in clothes, I should be convinced for these reasons, if experience had not taught me. The British soldiers are allowed eight pence sterling per day, with many necessaries that ours are not, and can buy what is requisite upon the cheapest terms; and they lie one half the year in camp or garrison, when they cannot consume the fifth part of what ours do in continual marches over mountains, rocks, and rivers. . . . And I dare say you will be candid enough to allow that few men would choose to have their lives exposed to the incessant insults of a merciless enemy, without some view or hope of reward."

But his difficulties with regard to money and supplies were as nothing to those which he endured when seeking to raise men, and to control them. His recruiting officers were negligent. "Several officers," he writes at one time, "have been out six weeks, or two months, without getting a man, spending their time in all the gayety of pleasurable mirth, with their relations and friends; not attempting nor having a possible chance to recruit any but those who, out of their inclination to the service, will proffer themselves." At one time, when the Shenandoah Valley was in imminent danger from Indians, he called upon Lord Fairfax and other officers of the militia to put forth special efforts to bring together all the men they could raise for an expedition to go out and scour the country, and when the day came, after all the drumming and beating up of recruits, only fifteen appeared!

Nor, after he had his men, could he bring them under regular discipline. He had seen something of the order which prevailed under English officers, and it brought into stronger contrast the loose, independent ways of the Virginia militia, where the men had very little notion of obedience, and regarded an order as a request which they could attend to or not as suited their convenience. All this was exasperating enough to a high-spirited commander, who knew that no effective military work could be done when there was such a spirit, and Washington prevailed upon the legislature to enact a more stringent code of laws, which gave more power to the commander, and compelled the soldier to obey at risk of severe penalty. To accomplish this, he had to visit Williamsburg and labor with the members of the legislature individually.

There is no doubt that Washington had very troublesome material to make into soldiers, and that, as a young commander, he was incensed by their conduct, and ready to be very summary with them. As a military man, he was also greatly annoyed by the indifferent manner in which he was supported by the country people whom he was engaged in protecting. One reason lay in the peculiar life of Virginia. When an ignorant white man found himself under strict orders, he resented it, because he thought it placed him on a level with negro slaves. Then there was no class of intelligent, hard-working mechanics, from which soldiers could be drafted. The planters' sons were ready to be officers, but they did not care about being privates. The better men in the ranks were drawn from the hardy backwoodsmen, whose life was a free, self-reliant one. In fact, the stubborn burgesses and independent soldiers were made stubborn and independent by the life in America which several generations of planters and frontiersmen had been living. Washington was too near these people to understand this at the time, but we can see that his troublesome soldiers were the stuff out of which the fighting armies of the war for independence were made.

The old trouble between provincial officers and those appointed by the king continued; and Washington found himself balked in his plans by a little whipper-snapper of a captain, who was posted at Fort Cumberland and refused to take orders from him. Even the governor was timidly unwilling to sustain the commander-in-chief, and in order to set the matter at rest, for the case was one which involved much, Washington made a journey to Boston to consult with Governor Shirley, who at that time was at the head of all the British forces in America.

This journey of seven weeks, taken on horseback in the middle of winter, was the first which the young Virginian had taken to the northward. His route lay through Philadelphia, New York, New London, and Newport; and everywhere that he went he was received with great attention. He obtained without difficulty the support of Governor Shirley, and had a long and thorough conference with him upon the plans of the approaching campaign. In one thing, however, he was disappointed. He had hoped to obtain a commission from the governor, as the king's representative, making him an officer in the regular army. He sought this more than once, but never obtained it. So much the better, we think, for America. Had Washington received such a commission and risen to the position in the British army which his genius would have commanded, he might not have served against his country, but it is not likely that he would have served for it as he did.

Then he had unceasing trouble with Governor Dinwiddie. The governor was a fussy, opinionated man, who showed much zeal in the defense of Virginia, but not always a zeal according to knowledge. He was constantly proposing impracticable schemes, and it required great patience and ingenuity on the part of Washington to persuade the governor out of his plans without perpetually coming into open conflict with him. He learned the part of the wise man who goes around a difficulty if possible, rather than over it.

The position in which Washington stood during these three years was indeed a very trying one. He was expected to defend the western border of Virginia against the incursions of the Indians, aided by the French, who grew more audacious after the defeat of Braddock. Yet he had, as it were, neither men nor money at his command, and the governor and burgesses, to whom he looked for aid, were quarreling at the other end of the province. His neighbors and friends gave him some help, but there were only a few who really stood by him in all weathers. More than once he was on the point of resigning a position which brought him scarcely anything but disappointment; but he was prevented by the urgency of his friends and by the crying needs of the settlers on the frontiers. If he failed them, who would protect them? And so this young man of twenty-four kept his post and worked month after month to secure peace and safety for them. How strongly he felt may be seen by a letter which he wrote to Governor Dinwiddie at the time of their sorest need: —

"Your Honor may see to what unhappy straits the distressed inhabitants and myself are reduced. I am too little acquainted, Sir, with pathetic language to attempt a description of the people's distresses, though I have a generous soul, sensible of wrongs, and swelling for redress. But what can I do? I see their situation, know their danger, and participate in their sufferings, without having it in my power to give them further relief than uncertain promises. In short, I see inevitable destruction in so clear a light that, unless vigorous measures are taken by the Assembly, and speedy assistance sent from below, the poor inhabitants that are now in forts must unavoidably fall, while the remainder are flying before the barbarous foe. In fine, the melancholy situation of the people, the little prospect of assistance, the gross and scandalous abuses cast upon the officers in general, which is reflecting upon me in particular, for suffering misconduct of such extraordinary kinds, and the distant prospect, if any, of gaining honor and reputation in the service, — cause me to lament the hour that gave me a commission, and would induce me at any other time than this of imminent danger, to resign, without one hesitating moment, a command, from which I never expect to reap either honor or benefit; but, on the contrary, have almost an absolute certainty of incurring displeasure below [that is, at Williamsburg and in the older parts of the province], while the murder of helpless families may be laid to my account here. The supplicating tears of the women and the moving petitions of the men melt me into such deadly sorrow, that I solemnly declare, if I know my own mind, I could offer myself a willing sacrifice to the butchering enemy, provided that would contribute to the people's ease."

It is no wonder that the constant anxiety and hardship which he endured undermined his health, and that for four months he was obliged to give up his command and retire to Mount Vernon. Upon his recovery, a brighter prospect opened. Dinwiddie was recalled and a more sensible lieutenant-governor took his place. Best of all, Mr. Pitt, the great English statesman, took direction of affairs in England, and at once planned for the quick ending of the war with France. He thrust out inefficient generals, and put the armies in America into the hands of resolute, able men. He won over the colonies by a hearty interest in them, and by counting on the colonial forces in the coming campaigns. Then he pushed preparation for attacking the French in their strongholds.

Washington was overjoyed at the news of another movement against Fort Duquesne. Virginia raised two regiments to add to the British regulars, who were under the command of General Forbes. Washington was to be at the head of one of these regiments, while still retaining his position as commander-in-chief of the Virginia forces. He was in hearty accord with the English officers and with the new governor, and he was at last with men who understood his value and listened with respect to his judgment. It is a great moment in a young man's life when older men turn to him for counsel, and if he has won his knowledge by solid experience, he is not likely to have his head turned by such attention. Washington had borne neglect and misunderstanding; he had been left to work out his plans by himself, and had for nearly three years been learning to rely upon himself, since there was no one else on whom he could lean. So he had become strong, and other men now leaned on him.

He was kept busy for some time at Winchester, collecting men and material, and at last marched to Fort Cumberland at the head of his forces. The expedition against Fort Duquesne was a different affair from that undertaken by Braddock. A lesson had been learned, and Washington was in a position now, not only to advise, but to carry out plans. Braddock had refused to listen to his advice, but Forbes and the other officers not only listened, but gave him the lead in many things. Washington had seen the folly of Braddock's elaborate and cumbersome outfit, and had urged him to move more lightly equipped. Now he had his way, and he took advantage of his men's lack of regimental clothing to dress them like Indians. "If I were left to pursue my own inclinations," he wrote to the British commander, "I would not only order the men to adopt the Indian dress, but cause the officers to do it also, and be the first to set the example myself. Nothing but the uncertainty of obtaining the general approbation causes me to hesitate a moment to leave my regimentals at this place, and proceed as light as any Indian in the woods. It is an unbecoming dress, I own, for an officer; but convenience rather than show, I think, should be consulted." Fortunately he did not have to deal with a pedantic officer. His dress was approved and became very popular. It "takes very well here," wrote the British commander, "and, thank God, we see nothing but shirts and blankets."

It must not be supposed, however, that all now went smoothly. On the contrary, Washington had a bitter disappointment. The general, influenced by the advice of some interested persons, proposed to cut a new road through Pennsylvania to Fort Duquesne. Washington remonstrated with all his might. They already had the old road, over which troops could be transported quickly and the expedition be brought to a speedy close. His remonstrance was in vain, and again he had to use all his patience and self-command, as he saw foolish counsels prevail. He was able, however, to prevent General Forbes from dividing his forces and sending part by one road, and part by the other; and he never indulged in a petty sulking fit, because his advice was not followed, or showed one whit less determination to do his part. " I pray your interest most sincerely with the general," he wrote to Colonel Bouquet, of the regular army, " to get myself and my regiment included in the number" [of the advance troops]. "If any argument is needed to obtain this favor, I hope without vanity I may be allowed to say that, from long intimacy with these woods, and frequent scouting in them, my men are at least as well acquainted with all the passes and difficulties, as any troops that will be employed."

He had his way in this. He had his way also, though he cared less for that, in showing the folly of the course pursued in opening a new road. However, the expedition succeeded, for when the general reached Fort Duquesne, the French had withdrawn their forces to meet a demand elsewhere, and had burned the fort.

The English now took possession of that part of the country. People forgot the mistakes which had been made. A new fort was built and named Fort Pitt (whence came the modern name of Pittsburgh), and Washington led his men back to Winchester.

There was no longer any need of an army to be kept in the field, now that the French had been driven from the Ohio Valley, and Washington resigned his commission. He had given up any expectation of receiving a commission in the British army, and he had indeed no longer a desire to be a soldier by profession. As with his brother Lawrence before him, something now occurred in his life which made it easy for him to be a Virginia planter.

CHAPTER XII.

WASHINGTON AT MOUNT VERNON..

NEAR the end of May, 1758, Washington was ordered by the Quartermaster-General of the British forces to leave Winchester and make all haste to Williamsburg, there to explain to the governor and council in what a desperate condition the Virginia troops were as regarded clothing and equipments. The army was making ready for its expedition against Fort Duquesne, and so urgent was the case that the young commander-in-chief of the volunteers was sent on this errand. He was on horseback, for that was the only mode of travel, and accompanied by Billy Bishop, once the military servant of General Braddock, but, since the death of the general, the faithful servant of the young Virginian aid who had read the funeral service over his dead master.

The two men had reached Williams Ferry, on the Pamunkey River, and had crossed on the boat, when they met Mr. Chamberlayne, a Virginian gentleman living in the neighborhood. The hospitable planter insisted that Washington should at once go to his house. It was forenoon, and dinner would be served as usual, early, and after that Colonel Washington could go forward to Williamsburg, if go he must. Besides all that, there was a charming young widow at his house — Colonel Washington must have known her, the daughter of John Dandridge, and the wife of John Parke Custis. Virginia hospitality was hard to resist, and Washington yielded. He would stay to dinner if his host would let him hurry off immediately afterward.

Bishop was bidden to bring his master's horse around after dinner in good season, and Washington surrendered himself to his host. Dinner followed, and the afternoon went by, and Mr. Chamberlayne was in excellent humor, as he kept one eye on the restless horses at the door, and the other on his guests, the tall, Indian-like officer and the graceful, hazel-eyed, animated young widow. Sunset came, and still Washington lingered. Then Mr. Chamberlayne stoutly declared that no guest was ever permitted to leave his house after sunset. Mrs. Martha Custis was not the one to drive the soldier away, and so Bishop was bidden to take the horses back to the stable. Not till the next morning did the young colonel take his leave. Then he dispatched his business promptly at Williamsburg, and whenever he could get an hour dashed over to White House, where Mrs. Custis lived. So prompt was he about this business, also, that when he returned to Winchester he had the promise of the young widow that she would marry him as soon as the campaign was over.

So runs the story told by the grandson of Mrs. Custis, for when she married Washington, January 6, 1759, she had two children, a boy of six and a girl of four.

Washington took his wife and her little children home to Mount Vernon, which was his own, since Lawrence Washington's only child had died, and his widow had married again. Martha Custis added her own large property to her husband's, and Washington was now a rich man, with large estates and with plenty to occupy him if he would devote himself to the care of his property.

From the time of his marriage until his death, Washington wore a miniature portrait of his wife, hung from his neck by a gold chain. "My dear Patsy," he calls her in his letters, and he was never happier than when living with her in quiet at Mount Vernon. They never had son or daughter; but Washington loved dearly the boy and girl whom his wife brought to him. The girl died when she was sixteen; the boy grew up, married, and became the father of several children.

Washington was broken with grief when his wife's daughter died, and when the son died, he adopted as his own the orphan children whom John Custis left behind.

It was no light matter to be a Virginia planter,

when one had so high a standard of excellence as George Washington had. The main crop which he raised was tobacco, and the immediate attention which it required was only during a small part of the year; but, as we have seen, a successful planter was also a man of business, and really the governor of a little province. Many planters contented themselves with leaving the care of their estates and their negroes to overseers, while they themselves spent their time in visiting and receiving visits, in sports, and in politics. That was not Washington's way. He might easily have done so, for he had money enough; but such a life would have been very distasteful to a man who had undergone the hardships of a soldier, and had acquired habits of thoroughness and of love of work. It would have been no pleasure to Washington to be idle and self-indulgent, while seeing his fences tumbling down, and knowing that he was spending more money for everything than was necessary. The man who attends to his own affairs, and sees everything thriving under wise management, is the most contented man, and Washington's heart was in his work.

So he looked after everything himself. He rose early, often before light, when the days were short. He breakfasted lightly at seven in the summer and at eight in winter, and after breakfast was in the saddle visiting the different parts of his estate, and looking after any improvements he had ordered. He was a splendid horseman and very fond of breaking in new horses. Dinner followed at two o'clock; he had an early tea; and when living at home, he was often in bed by nine o'clock.

These were regular, old fashioned hours, and the life which he led enabled him to accomplish a vast amount. He kept no clerk, but wrote out in his large round hand all his letters and orders, entered every item in his day-book and ledger, and was scrupulously exact about every farthing of his accounts. He did not guess how he stood at any time, but he knew precisely how last year's crop compared with this year's; how many head of cattle he had; how many acres he had planted with tobacco; what wood he had cut; and just what goods he had ordered from London. He had been appointed by the court, guardian of his wife's two children, who had inherited property from their father; and he kept all their accounts separate, with the minutest care, for he held a trust to be sacred.

Twice a year he sent to his agent in London a list of such articles as he needed; there were plows, hoes, spades, and other agricultural implements; drugs, groceries of various sorts, clothes both for his family and for his negroes; tools, books, busts, and ornaments; household furniture, and linen. Indeed, as one reads the long invoices which Washington sent to London, he wonders how people managed who had to send across the Atlantic for everything they might possibly need for the next six months. Then there were special orders for the children; for "Master Custis, six years old," there were, besides Irish holland, fine cambric, gloves, shoes, stockings, hats, combs, and brushes, such items as these, — "one pair handsome silver shoe and knee buckles, ten shillings' worth of toys, and six little books, for children beginning to read;" while for "Miss Custis, four years old," were a great variety of clothes, including "two caps, two pairs of ruffles, two tuckers, bibs, and aprons if fashionable," and finally, a "fashionable dressed baby, ten shillings, and other toys" to the same amount.

He required his agent to send him, with his bill for all the goods, the original bills of the merchants who sold the goods to the agent; then he copied all these orders and bills, giving every item, and in this way he had before him in his books an exact statement, in every particular, of his transactions.

He watched the market closely, and knew just what the varying price of tobacco was, and what he might expect for any other goods which he sent to be sold. He was determined that everything from his plantation should be of value and should receive its full price. So high a reputation did he secure for honesty that it was said that any barrel of flour that bore the brand of George

Washington, Mount Vernon, was exempted from the customary inspection in the West Indian ports.

Like other Virginia planters, Washington was a slave-holder. All the work on the plantations was done by slaves, and no other method was supposed possible. Washington was born into a society where slaves were held as a matter of course, and he inherited slaves. At that time the right to own negroes was scarcely questioned, and slaves were held throughout the colonies. There are few things that test the character of a man more than his treatment of those who are dependent upon him, — his servants, his workmen, his children. Washington was a just and a generous master. He cared for his slaves, not merely because to have them well and strong was more profitable, but because without his care they would suffer. He looked after them in their sickness because he was humane and compassionate. He also required good work of them. That was what they were for — to work; and he knew each man's capacity. He watched them at their work, and as they would labor more industriously when he was looking on, he made up his mind what they could do, and then expected just so much from them. But he was fair in all this; he made allowances for different kinds of work, and tried to be perfectly just in his requirements.

He even worked with his men, and that was a

rare thing for a Virginia planter to do. He kept a diary of his occupation, so that we can follow the farmer day after day.

This is the busy planter, with his hands full of work; but there was another kind of life going on, not in the quarters, or the field, but in the house. On rainy days, Washington took down his ledger and posted it, and worked over his accounts, but he was also the hospitable gentleman who opened his doors wide to guests. Not only the neighboring families, the Fairfaxes, and others came and went, but the man who had been commander-in-chief of the Virginia army and the best-known military man in America, was sure to be visited by every one of distinction who passed that way. The governors of Virginia and Maryland were his guests; and he himself with his beautiful wife were welcomed at Williamsburg and Annapolis and the country-seats of the most notable people.

He was extremely fond of society. A grave, silent man himself, he was very gallant and courtly, and in those days moved through the stately minuet with a fine air. He admired beautiful women, and he liked to listen to good talkers; he rarely laughed loudly, but he had a sly amusement over ludicrous things; and while he kept most people at a distance by his serious manners, he had the love of children and young people. After all, his greatest pleasure was in those sports which were akin to work and to that military life which had been his passion. He was always ready for a fox-hunt. As in his younger days he had ridden with Lord Fairfax and the Fairfaxes of Belvoir, so now, when he was master of Mount Vernon, he and his friends were always out in the season, and when night came, the party would meet at one house or the other, for a merry supper, to be off again behind the hounds early the next day.

In a letter describing Mount Vernon, Washington speaks of it as "on one of the finest rivers in the world; a river well stocked with various kinds of fish, at all seasons of the year, and in the spring with shad, herring, bass, carp, sturgeon, etc., in great abundance. The borders of the estate are washed by more than ten miles of tide-water; several valuable fisheries appertain to it; the whole shore, in fact, is one entire fishery." Here was business and sport combined, and it was a great occasion in the herring season, when the fish came up in vast shoals, and the negroes turned out to haul in the seine with its catch. In the season of canvas-back ducks, also, Washington was out with his fowling-piece early and late. The story is told that he had been much annoyed by a lawless fellow who came without leave to shoot on the estate. He crossed over from the Maryland shore, and hid his boat in one of the creeks. One day Washington heard the report of a gun, and guessing it to be that of this man, who had more than once been warned to leave, he sprang on his horse and rode in the direction of the sound. He pushed his way through the bushes just as the man, who had seen him approach, was pushing his boat off. The trespasser raised his gun, and aimed it at Washington, who spurred his horse at once into the water and seized the boat before the man knew what he was about. Then Washington, who had a powerful arm, seized the fellow and gave him a sound thrashing, and was never troubled by him again.

There was always a Washington to surprise people. There was the still, self-controlled, grave man, who suddenly flashed forth in a resolute act, seizing the opportunity, and doing the one thing which was instantly demanded; and there was the quick-tempered, fiery man who held himself in check, waited for other people to speak and act, and then came forward with a few plain, deliberate words, which showed that he had grasped the whole situation, and could be depended on to carry through his resolution patiently and persistently.

There were, as I have said, few towns in Virginia. The divisions were by parishes, after the old English custom, and so when a man was of importance in his neighborhood he was very apt to be a vestryman in his parish. Mount Vernon was in Truro parish, and Washington was a vestryman there, as also in Fairfax parish. It happened that the church of Truro parish had fallen into decay, and was in a sorry condition. It was necessary to build a new one, and several meetings were held, for two parties had sprung up, one wishing to rebuild on the same spot; and another urging some location more convenient to the parishioners, for the place where the old church had stood was not a central one. Finally a meeting was called to settle the matter. One of Washington's friends, George Mason, a man of fine speech, rose up and spoke most eloquently in favor of holding to the old site; there their fathers had worshiped, and there had their bodies been laid to rest. Every one seemed moved and ready to accept Mason's proposal.

Washington had also come prepared with a plea. He had not Mason's power of speech, but he took from his pocket a roll of paper and spread it before the meeting. On this sheet he had drawn off a plan of Truro parish; upon the plan were marked plainly the site of the old church, the place where every parishioner lived, and the spot which he advised as the site for the new church. He said very little; he simply showed the people his survey, and let them see for themselves that every consideration of convenience and fairness pointed to the new site as the one to be chosen. It was central, and no one could fail to see that the church was first of all for the living. His argument was the argument of good sense and reasonableness, and it carried the day against Mason's eloquent speech. Pohick Church, which was built on the new site, was constructed from plans which Washington himself drew.

CHAPTER XIII.

A VIRGINIA BURGESS.

BEFORE Washington's marriage, and while he was in camp near Fort Cumberland, making active preparations for the campaign against Fort Duquesne, there was an election for members of the Virginia House of Burgesses. Washington offered himself as candidate to the electors of Frederick County, in which Winchester, where he had been for the past three years, was the principal town. His friends were somewhat fearful that the other candidates, who were on the ground, would have the advantage over Washington, who was with the army, at a distance; and they wrote, urging him to come on and look after his interests. Colonel Bouquet, under whose orders he was, cheerfully gave him leave of absence, but Washington replied: —

"I had, before Colonel Stephen came to this place, abandoned all thoughts of attending personally the election at Winchester, choosing rather to leave the management of that affair to my friends, than be absent from my regiment, when there is a probability of its being called to duty. I am much pleased now, that I did so."

Here was a case where Washington broke his excellent rule of — "If you want a thing done, do it yourself." If his regiment was to lie idle at Fort Cumberland, he could easily have galloped to Winchester, and have been back in a few days; but there was a chance that it might move, and so he gave up at once all thought of leaving it. Glad enough he was to have the news confirmed. To lead his men forward, and to have a hand in the capture of Fort Duquesne, was the first thing — the election must take care of itself. This was not a bad statement for his friends at Winchester to make. A man who sticks to his post, and does his duty without regard to his personal interests, is the very man for a representative in the legislature. The people of Frederick knew Washington thoroughly, and though they had sometimes felt his heavy hand, they gave him a hearty vote, and he was elected a member of the House of Burgesses.

This was in 1758, and he continued to serve as a member for the next fifteen years. There is a story told of his first appearance in the House. He was something more than a new member; he was the late commander-in-chief of the Virginia army, the foremost man, in a military way, in the province; he had just returned from the successful expedition against Fort Duquesne. So the House resolved to welcome him in a manner becoming so gallant a Virginian, and it passed a vote of thanks for the distinguished military services he had rendered the country. The Speaker, Mr. Robinson, rose when Washington came in to take his seat, and made a little speech of praise and welcome, presenting the thanks of the House. Every one applauded and waited for the tall colonel to respond. There he stood, blushing, stammering, confused. He could give his orders to his men easily enough, and he could even say what was necessary to Mrs. Martha Custis; but to address the House of Burgesses in answer to a vote of thanks — that was another matter! Not a plain word could he get out. It was a capital answer, and the Speaker interpreted it to the House.

"Sit down, Mr. Washington," said he. "Your modesty equals your valor, and that surpasses the power of any language I possess."

It was a trying ordeal for the new member, and if speech-making had been his chief business in the House, he would have made a sorry failure. He rarely made a speech, and never a long one, but for all that he was a valuable member, and his reëlection at every term showed that the people understood his value. If there was any work to be done, any important committee to be appointed, Washington could be counted on, and his sound judgment, his mature experience, and sense of honor, made his opinion one which every one respected. He was always on hand, punctual, and faithful; and qualities of diligence and fidelity in such a place, when combined with sound judgment and honor, are sure to tell in the long run. He once gave a piece of advice to a nephew who had also been elected to the House, and it probably was the result of his own experience and observation.

"The only advice I will offer," he said, "if you have a mind to command the attention of the House, is to speak seldom but on important subjects, except such as particularly relate to your constituents; and, in the former case, make yourself perfect master of the subject. Never exceed a decent warmth, and submit your sentiments with diffidence. A dictatorial style, though it may carry conviction, is always accompanied with disgust."

It was in January, 1759, that Washington took his seat in the House, and if he made it his rule "to speak seldom but on important subjects," he had several opportunities to speak before he finally left the Virginia legislature for a more important gathering. The first very important subject was the Stamp Act, in 1765. The British government had passed an act requiring the American colonies to place a stamp upon every newspaper or almanac that was published, upon every marriage certificate, every will, every deed, and upon other legal papers. These stamps were to be sold by officers of the crown, and the money obtained by the sale was to be used to pay British soldiers stationed in America to enforce the laws made by Parliament.

The colonies were aflame with indignation. They declared that Parliament had no right to pass such an act; that the Ministry that proposed it was about an unlawful business; and that it was adding insult to injury to send over soldiers to enforce such laws. People, when they meet on the corner of the street and discuss public matters, are usually much more outspoken than when they meet in legislatures; but the American colonists were wont to talk very plainly in their assemblies, and it was no new thing for the representatives, chosen by the people, to be at odds with the governor, who represented the British government. So when Patrick Henry rose in the House of Burgesses, with his resolutions declaring that the Stamp Act was illegal, and that the colony of Virginia had always enjoyed the right of governing itself, as far as taxation went, — and when he made a flaming speech which threatened the king, there was great confusion; and though his resolutions were passed, there was but a bare majority.

There is no record of what Washington may have said or how he voted on that occasion, but his letters show that he thought the Stamp Act a very unwise proceeding on the part of Great Britain, and a piece of oppression. "That act," he says, " could be looked upon in no other light by every person who would view it in its proper colors." But he did not rush into a passion over it. Instead, he studied it coolly, and before it was repealed wrote at some length to his wife's uncle, who was living in London, his reasons for thinking that the British ministry would gain nothing by pressing the Stamp Act and other laws which bore hard on colonial prosperity; for he held that if they would only see it, the colonies were as necessary to England as England was to the colonies.

It is difficult for us to-day to put ourselves in the place of Washington and other men of his time. Washington was a Virginian, and was one of the legislature. He was used to making laws and providing for the needs of the people of Virginia, but he was accustomed to look beyond Virginia to England. There the king was, and he was one of the subjects of the king. The king's officers came to Virginia, and when Washington saw, as he so often did, a British man-of-war lying in the river off Mount Vernon, his mind was thrilled with pleasure as he thought of the power of the empire to which he belonged. He had seen the British soldiers marching against the French, and he had himself served under a British general. He had an ardent desire to go to England, to see London, to see the king and his court, and Parliament, and the Courts of Justice, and the great merchants who made the city famous; but as yet he had been unable to go.

He had seen but little of the other colonies. He had made a journey to Boston, and that had given him some acquaintance with men; but wherever he went, he found people looking eagerly toward England and asking what the ministry there would do about fighting the French on the Western borders. Though he and others might never have seen England, it was the centre of the world to them. He thought of the other colonies not so much as all parts of one great country on this side of the Atlantic, as each separately a part of the British Empire.

After all, however, and most of all, he was a Virginian. In Virginia he owned land. There was his home, and there his occupation. He was a farmer, a planter of tobacco and wheat, and it was his business to sell his products. As for the French, they were enemies of Great Britain, but they were also very near enemies of Virginia. They were getting possession of land in Virginia itself — land which Washington owned in part; and when he was busily engaged in driving them out, he did not have to stop and think of France, he needed only to think of Fort Duquesne, a few days' march to the westward.

When, therefore he found the British government making laws which made him pay roundly for sending his tobacco to market, and taxing him as if there were no Virginia legislature to say what taxes the people could and should pay, he began to be restless and dissatisfied. England was a great way off; Virginia was close at hand. He was loyal to the king and had fought under the king's officers, but if the king cared nothing for his loyalty, and only wanted his pence, his loyalty was likely to cool. His chief resentment, however, was against Parliament. Parliament was making laws and laying taxes. But what was Parliament? It was a body of law-makers in England, just as the House of Burgesses was in Virginia. To be sure, it could pass laws about navigation which concerned all parts of the British Empire; but, somehow, it made these laws very profitable to England and very disadvantageous to Virginia. Parliament, however, had no right to pass such a law as the Stamp Act. That was making a special law for the American colonies, and taking away a right which belonged to the colonial assemblies.

Washington had grown up with an intense love of law, and in this he was like other American Englishmen. In England there were very few persons who made the laws, the vast majority had nothing to do but to obey the laws. Yet it is among the makers of laws that the love of law prevails; and since in America a great many more Englishmen had to do with government in colony and in town than in England, there were more who passionately insisted upon the law being observed. An unlawful act was to them an outrage.

When they said that England was oppressing them, and making them slaves, they did not mean that they wanted liberty to do what they pleased, but that they wanted to be governed by just laws, made by the men who had the right to make laws. And that right belonged to the legislatures, to which they sent representatives.

So it was out of his love of law and justice that Washington and others protested against the Stamp Act; and when the act was repealed they threw up their hats and hurrahed, not because they now should not have to buy and use stamps, but because by repealing the act Parliament had as much as said that it was an unlawful act. However, this was an unwilling admission on the part of Parliament, which repealed the act, but said at once: "We can tax you if we choose to."

In fact, Parliament stupidly tried soon after to prove that it had the right by imposing duties on tea, paper, glass, and painters' colors. But the people in the colonies were on the alert. They had really been governing themselves so long that now, when Parliament tried to get the power away from them, they simply went on using their power. They did this in two ways; the colonial governments again asserted their rights in the case, and the people began to form associations, in which they bound themselves not to buy goods of England until the offensive act was repealed. This latter was one of the most interesting movements in the breaking away of the colonies from England. It was a popular movement; it did not depend upon what this or that colonial assembly might do; it was perfectly lawful, and so far as it was complete it was effective. Yet all the while the movement was doing more, and what but a very few detected; it was binding the scattered people in the colonies together.

Washington took a great deal of interest in these associations, and belonged to one himself. He was growing exceedingly impatient of English misrule, and saw clearly to what it was leading. "At a time," he says, "when our lordly masters in Great Britain will be satisfied with nothing less than the deprivation of American freedom, it seems highly necessary that something should be done to avert the stroke, and maintain the liberty which we have derived from our ancestors. But the manner of doing it to answer the purpose effectually is the point in question. That no man should scruple, or hesitate a moment, to use arms in defense of so valuable a blessing, is clearly my opinion. Yet arms, I would beg leave to add, should be the last resort. We have already, it is said, proved the inefficacy of addresses to the throne, and remonstrances to Parliament. How far, then, their attention to our rights and privileges is to be awakened or alarmed by starving their trade and manufactures remains to be tried."

He took the lead in forming an association in

Virginia, and he kept scrupulously to his agreement; for when he sent his orders to London, he was very careful to instruct his correspondents to send him none of the goods unless the Act of Parliament had meantime been repealed. As the times grew more exciting, Washington watched events steadily. He took no step backward, but he moved forward deliberately and with firmness. He did not allow himself to be carried away by the passions of the time. It was all very well, some said, to stop buying from England, but let us stop selling also. They need our tobacco. Suppose we refuse to send it unless Parliament repeals the act. Washington stood out against that except as a final resource, and for the reason which he stated in a letter: —

"I am convinced, as much as I am of my own existence, that there is no relief for us but in their distress; and I think, at least I hope, that there is public virtue enough left among us to deny ourselves everything but the bare necessaries of life to accomplish this end. This we have a right to do, and no power upon earth can compel us to do otherwise, till it has first reduced us to the most abject state of slavery. The stopping of our exports would, no doubt, be a shorter method than the other to effect this purpose; but if we owe money to Great Britain, nothing but the last necessity can justify the non-payment of it; and, therefore, I have great doubts upon this head, and wish to see the other method first tried, which is legal and will facilitate these payments."

That is, by the economy necessarily preached, the people would save money with which to pay their debts.

Washington had been at the front in the House of Burgesses, in his own county, and among the people generally. He was a member of the convention called to meet at Williamsburg; and he was appointed by that convention one of seven delegates to attend the first Continental Congress at Philadelphia.

CHAPTER XIV.

THE CONTINENTAL CONGRESS.

NEAR the end of August, 1774, Patrick Henry and Edmund Pendleton, two of the delegates from Virginia to the first Continental Congress, rode from their homes to Mount Vernon and made a short visit. Then, on the last day of the month, Washington mounted his horse also, and the three friends started for Philadelphia to attend the Congress, which was called to meet on the 5th of September. Pendleton was a dozen years older than Washington, and Henry was the youngest of the party. He was the most fiery in speech, and more than once, in recent conventions, had carried his hearers away by his bold words. He was the most eloquent man in the colonies, — of rude appearance, but when once wrought up by excitement, able to pour out a torrent of words.

For my part, I would rather have heard the speech which Washington made at the convention in Williamsburg in the August before, when he rose to read the resolution which he and his neighbors had passed at their meeting in Fairfax County. The eloquence of a man who is a famous orator is not quite so convincing as that of a man of action, who rarely speaks, but who is finally stirred by a great occasion. People were used to hearing Washington say a few words in a slow, hesitating, deliberate way; and they knew that he had carefully considered beforehand what words he should use. But this time he was terribly in earnest, and when he had read the resolution, he spoke as no one had heard him before. He was a passionate man, who had his anger under control; but when it occasionally burst out, it was as if a dam to a stream had given way. And now he was consumed with indignation at the manner in which Great Britain was treating the colonies. He was ready, he said, to raise a regiment of a thousand men, pay all their expenses, and lead them to Boston to drive out the king's soldiers.

The three men, therefore, must have talked long and earnestly as they rode to Philadelphia; for the Congress which they were to attend was the first one to which all the colonies were invited to send delegates. It was to consider the cause of the whole people, and Virginia was to see in Massachusetts not a rival colony, but one with which she had common cause. The last time Washington had gone over the road he had been on an errand to the king's chief representative in America, the commander-in-chief, Governor Shirley, and one matter which he had held very much at heart had been his own commission as an officer in his Majesty's army. He was on a different errand now. Still, like the men who were most in earnest at that time, he was thinking how the colonies could secure their rights as colonies, not how they might break away from England and set up for themselves.

They were five days on the road, and on September the 4th they breakfasted near New Castle, in Delaware, dined at Chester, in Pennsylvania, and in the evening were in Philadelphia, at the City Tavern, which stood on Second Street, above Walnut Street, and was the meeting-place of most of the delegates. Washington, however, though he was often at the City Tavern, had his lodging at Dr. Shippen's. The Congress met the next day at Carpenters' Hall, and was in session for seven weeks. The first two or three days were especially exciting to the members. There they were, fifty-one men, from all the colonies save Georgia, met to consult together — Englishmen who sang "God save the king," but asked also what right the king had to act as he had done toward Boston. They did not know one another well at the beginning. There was no man among them who could be called famous beyond his own colony, unless it were George Washington. Up to this time the different colonies had lived so apart from one another, each concerned about its own affairs, that there had been little opportunity for a man to be widely known.

So, as they looked at one another at the City

Tavern, or at Carpenters' Hall when they met, each man was wondering who would take the lead. Virginia was the largest and most important colony. Massachusetts had a right to speak, because she had called the convention, and because it was in Boston that the people were suffering most from the action of the British Parliament. Perhaps the two most conspicuous members at first were Patrick Henry of Virginia, and Samuel Adams of Massachusetts; but in the seven weeks of the session, others showed their good judgment and patriotism. Patrick Henry was asked after he returned to Virginia whom he considered the greatest man in the Congress, and he replied: " If you speak of eloquence, Mr. Rutledge of South Carolina is by far the greatest orator; but if you speak of solid information and sound judgment, Colonel Washington is unquestionably the greatest man on the floor."

Washington carried on the methods which he had always practiced. He attended the sessions punctually and regularly; he listened to what others had to say, and gave his own opinion only after he had carefully formed it. It is an example of the thoroughness with which he made himself master of every subject, that he used to copy in his own hand the important papers which were laid before Congress, such as the petition to the king which was agreed upon. This he would do deliberately and exactly, — it was like committing the paper to memory. Besides this, he made abstracts of other papers, stating the substance of them in a few clear words.

The greater part of each day was occupied in the Congress, but besides the regular business, there was a great deal of informal talk among the members. They were full of the subject, and used to meet to discuss affairs at dinner, or in knots about the fire at the City Tavern. Philadelphia was then the most important city in the country, and there were many men of wide experience living in it. Washington went everywhere by invitation. He dined with the Chief Justice, with the Mayor, and with all the notable people.

In this way he was able to become better acquainted both with the state of affairs in other colonies and with the way the most intelligent people were thinking about the difficulties of the time. The first Continental Congress gave expression to the deliberate judgment of the colonies upon the acts of Great Britain. It protested against the manner in which Parliament was treating the colonies. It declared firmly and solemnly that as British subjects the people of the colonies owed no allegiance to Parliament, in which they had no representatives; that their own legislatures alone had the right to lay taxes. But after all, the great advantage of this first Congress was in the opportunity which it gave for representatives from the different colonies to become acquainted with one another, and thus to make all parts of the country more ready to act together.

It was only now and then that any one suggested the independence of the colonies. Washington, like a few others, thought it possible the colonies might have to arm and resist the unlawful attempt to force unconstitutional laws upon them; but he did not, at this time, go so far as to propose a separation from England. He had a friend among the British officers in Boston, one of his old comrades in the war against France, a Captain Mackenzie, who wrote to him, complaining of the way the Boston people were behaving. Captain Mackenzie, very naturally, as an officer, saw only a troublesome, rebellious lot of people whom it was the business of the army to put down. Washington wrote earnestly to him, trying to show him the reason why the people felt as they did, and the wrong way of looking at the subject which Captain Mackenzie and other officers had. He expressed his sorrow that fortune should have placed his friend in a service that was sure to bring down vengeance upon those engaged in it. He went on:

"I do not mean by this to insinuate that an officer is not to discharge his duty, even when chance, not choice, has placed him in a disagreeable situation; but I conceive, when you condemn the conduct of the Massachusetts people, you reason from effects, not causes; otherwise you would not wonder at a people, who are every day receiving fresh proofs of a systematic assertion of an arbitrary power, deeply planned to overturn the laws and constitution of their country, and to violate the most essential and valuable rights of mankind, being irritated, and with difficulty restrained from acts of the greatest violence and intemperance. For my own part, I confess to you candidly, that I view things in a very different point of light from the one in which you seem to consider them; and though you are taught by venal men . . . to believe that the people of Massachusetts are rebellious, setting up for independency, and what not, give me leave, my good friend, to tell you, that you are abused, grossly abused. . . . Give me leave to add, and I think I can announce it as a fact, that it is not the wish or interest of that government, or any other upon this continent, separately or collectively, to set up for independence; but this you may at the same time rely on, that none of them will ever submit to the loss of those valuable rights and privileges which are essential to the happiness of every free state, and without which, life, liberty, and property are rendered totally insecure."

It was with such a belief as this that Washington went back to Mount Vernon, and while he was occupied with his engrossing private affairs, busied himself also with organizing and drilling soldiers. Independent companies were formed all over Virginia, and one after another placed themselves under his command. Although, by the custom of those companies, each was independent of the others, yet by choosing the same commander they virtually made Washington commander-in-chief of the Virginia volunteers. He was the first military man in the colony, and every one turned to him for advice and instruction. So through the winter and spring he was constantly on the move, going to one place after another to review the companies which had been formed.

I think that winter and spring of 1775 must have been a somewhat sorrowful one to George Washington, and that he must have felt as if a great change were coming in his life. His wife's daughter had died, and he missed her sadly. Young John Custis had married and gone away to live. The sound of war was heard on all sides, and among the visitors to Mount Vernon were some who afterward were to be generals in the American army. He still rode occasionally after the hounds, but the old days of fun were gone. George William Fairfax had gone back to England, and the jolly company at Belvoir was scattered. The house itself there had caught fire and burned to the ground.

But the time for action was at hand. Washington turned from his home and his fox-hunting to go to Richmond as a delegate to a second Virginia convention. It was called to hear the reports of the delegates to Philadelphia and to see what further was to be done. It was clear to some, and to Washington among them, that the people must be ready for the worst. They had shown themselves in earnest by all the training they had been going through as independent companies. Now let those companies be formed into a real army. It was idle to send any more petitions to the king.

"We must fight!" exclaimed Patrick Henry; "I repeat it, sir; we must fight! An appeal to arms and the God of Hosts is all that is left us!"

A committee, of which Washington was one, was appointed to report a plan for an army of Virginia.

But when people make up their minds to fight, they know very well, if they are sensible, that more than half the task before them is to find means for feeding and clothing not only the troops but the people who are dependent on the troops. Therefore the convention appointed another committee, of which Washington also was a member, to devise a plan for encouraging manufactures, so that the people could do without England. Heretofore, the Virginians had done scarcely any manufacturing; nearly everything they needed they had bought from England with tobacco. But if they were to be at war with England, they must be making ready to provide for themselves. It was late in the day to do anything; slavery, though they did not then see it clearly, had made a variety of industries impossible. However, the people were advised to form associations to promote the raising of wool, cotton, flax, and hemp, and to encourage the use of home manufactures.

Washington was again chosen one of the delegates to the Continental Congress, for the second Congress had been called to meet at Philadelphia. He was even readier to go than before. On the day when he was chosen, he wrote to his brother John Augustine Washington: "It is my full intention to devote my life and fortune to the cause we are engaged in, if needful."

That was at the end of March. The second Continental Congress was to meet on May 10; and just before Washington left Mount Vernon came the news of Lexington and Concord. Curiously enough, the governor of Virginia had done just what Governor Gage had attempted to do; he had seized some powder which was stored at Fredericksburg, and placed it for safety on board a vessel of the British navy. The independent companies at once met and called upon Washington to take command of them, that they might compel the governor to restore the powder. Washington kept cool. The governor promised to restore the powder, and Washington advised the people to wait to see what Congress would do.

When Congress met, the men who came together were no longer strangers to one another. They had parted warm friends the previous fall; they had gone to their several homes and now had come back more determined than ever, and more united. Every one spoke of Lexington and Concord; and the Massachusetts men told how large an army had already gathered around Boston. But it was an army made up not only of Massachusetts men, but of men from Connecticut, Rhode Island, and New Hampshire. It was plain that there must be some authority over such an army, and the Provincial Congress of Massachusetts wrote to the Continental Congress at Philadelphia, advising that body to assume control of all the forces, to raise a continental army, appoint a commander, and do whatever else was necessary to prepare for war. There had already been fighting; there was an army; and it was no longer a war between Massachusetts and Great Britain.

I do not know what other delegates to the Congress at Philadelphia came as soldiers, but there was one tall Virginian present who wore his military coat; and when the talk fell upon appointing a commander, all eyes were turned toward him. Every one, however, felt the gravity and delicacy of the situation. Here was an army adopted by Congress; but it was a New England army, and if the struggle were to come at Boston, it was natural that the troops should mainly come from that neighborhood. The colonies were widely separated; they had not acted much together. Would it not be better, would it not save ill-feeling, if a New England man were to command this New England army?

There were some who thought thus; and besides, there was still a good deal of difference of opinion as to the course to be pursued. Some were ready for independence; others, and perhaps the most, hoped to bring the British to terms. Parties were rising in Congress; petty jealousies were showing themselves, when suddenly John Adams of Massachusetts, seeing into what perplexities they were drifting, came forward with a distinct proposition that Congress should adopt the army before Boston and appoint a commander. He did not name Washington, but described him as a certain gentleman from Virginia "who could unite the cordial exertions of all the colonies better than any other person." No one doubted who was meant, and Washington, confused and agitated, left the room at once.

Nothing else was now talked of. The delegates discussed the matter in groups and small circles, and a few days afterward a Maryland delegate formally nominated George Washington to be commander-in-chief of the American army. He was unanimously elected, but the honor of bringing him distinctly before the Congress belongs to John Adams. It seems now a very natural thing to do, but really it was something which required wisdom and courage. When one sums up all Washington's military experience at this time, it was not great, or such as to point him out as unmistakably the leader of the American army. There was a general then in command at Cambridge, who had seen more of war than Washington had. But

Washington was the leading military man in Virginia, and it was for this reason that John Adams, as a New England man, urged his election. The Congress had done something to bring the colonies together; the war was to do more, but probably no single act really had a more far-reaching significance in making the Union, than the act of nominating the Virginian Washington by the New England Adams.

CHAPTER XV.

UNDER THE OLD ELM.

IT was on the 15th day of June, 1775, that George Washington was chosen commander-in-chief of the American army. The next day he made his answer to Congress, in which he declared that he accepted the office, but that he would take no pay; he would keep an exact account of his expenses, but he would give his services to his country. There was no time to be lost. He could not go home to bid his wife goodby, and he did not know when he would see her again, so he wrote her as follows : —

"PHILADELPHIA, 18*th June*, 1775.

"MY DEAREST: I am now set down to write to you on a subject which fills me with inexpressible concern, and this concern is greatly aggravated and increased when I reflect upon the uneasiness I know it will give you. It has been determined in Congress that the whole army raised for the defense of the American cause shall be put under my care, and that it is necessary for me to proceed immediately to Boston to take upon me the command of it.

"You may believe me, my dear Patsy, when I assure you in the most solemn manner, that, so far from seeking this appointment, I have used every endeavor in my power to avoid it, not only from my unwillingness to part with you and the family, but from a consciousness of it being a trust too great for my capacity, and that I should enjoy more real happiness in one month with you at home than I have the most distant prospect of finding abroad, if my stay were to be seven times seven years. But, as it has been a kind of destiny that has thrown me upon this service, I shall hope that my undertaking it is designed to answer some good purpose. You might, and I suppose did perceive, from the tenor of my letters, that I was apprehensive I could not avoid this appointment, as I did not pretend to intimate when I should return. That was the case. It was utterly out of my power to refuse this appointment, without exposing my character to such censures as would have reflected dishonor upon myself and given pain to my friends."

That is to say, he could not refuse the appointment without laying himself open to the charge of being a coward and afraid to run the risk, or a selfish man who preferred his own ease and comfort. He was neither. He was a courageous man, as he had always shown himself to be, and he was unselfish, for he was giving up home and property, and undertaking a life of the greatest difficulty in the service of — what? His country? Yes. But we must remember that Virginia was his country more than all the colonies were, and at present it was only Massachusetts that stood in peril. Of course every one is impelled to do great things by more than one motive. Washington was a soldier, and his blood tingled as he thought of being commander-in-chief, and doing the most that a soldier could; but he was, above all, a man who had a keen sense of right and wrong. He saw that England was wrong and was doing injustice to America. The injustice did not at once touch him as a planter, as a man who was making money; it touched him as a free man who was obedient to the laws; and he was ready to give up everything to help right the wrongs.

Washington left Philadelphia on his way to Boston, June 21, escorted by a troop of horsemen, and accompanied by Schuyler and Lee, who had just been made major-generals by Congress. They had gone about twenty miles when they saw a man on horseback coming rapidly down the road. It was a messenger riding post-haste to Philadelphia, and carrying to Congress news of the battle of Bunker Hill. Everybody was stirred by the news and wanted to know the particulars.

"Why were the Provincials compelled to retreat?" he was asked.

"It was for want of ammunition," he replied.

"Did they stand the fire of the regular troops?" asked Washington anxiously.

"That they did, and held their own fire in reserve until the enemy was within eight rods."

"Then the liberties of the country are safe!"

exclaimed Washington. He remembered well the scenes under Braddock, and he knew what a sight it must have been to those New England farmers when a compact body of uniformed soldiers came marching up from the boats at Charlestown. If they could stand fearlessly, there was stuff in them to make soldiers of.

All along the route the people in the towns turned out to see Washington's cavalcade, and at Newark a committee of the New York Provincial Congress met to escort him to the city. There he left General Schuyler in command, and hurried forward to Cambridge, for the news of Bunker Hill made him extremely anxious to reach the army.

In New England, the nearer he came to the seat of war, the more excited and earnest he found the people. At every town he was met by the citizens and escorted through that place to the next. This was done at New Haven. The collegians all turned out, and they had a small band of music, at the head of which, curiously enough, was a freshman who afterward made some stir in the world. It was Noah Webster, the man of spelling-book and dictionary fame. At Springfield, the party was met by a committee of the Provincial Congress of Massachusetts, and at last, on the 2d of July, he came to Watertown, where he was welcomed by the Provincial Congress itself, which was in session there.

It was about two o'clock in the afternoon of the same day that Washington rode into Cambridge, escorted by a company of citizens. As he drew near Cambridge Common, cannon were fired to welcome him, and the people in Boston must have wondered what had happened. The Provincial Congress had set apart for his use the house of the president of Harvard College, reserving only one room for the president; but this house was probably too small and inconvenient; for shortly afterward Washington was established in the great square house, on the way to Watertown, which had been deserted by a rich Tory, and there he stayed as long as he was in Cambridge. By good fortune, years afterward, the poet Longfellow bought the house, and so the names of Washington and Longfellow have made it famous.

On the morning of the next day, which was Monday, July 3, 1775, Washington, with Lee and other officers, rode into camp. Cambridge Common was not the little place it now is, hemmed in by streets. It stretched out toward the country, and a country road ran by its side, leading to Watertown. An Episcopal church stood opposite the Common, and a little farther on, just as the road turned, nearly at a right angle, stood an old house. In front of this house, at the corner of the road, was a stout elm-tree. It was a warm summer morning, and the officers were glad of the shade of the tree.

On the left, and stretching behind, were the tents of the American camp. The soldiers themselves were drawn up in the road and on the dry, treeless common. Crowded about were men, women, and children, for the news had spread that the general had come, and the crowd and the soldiers were well intermingled. What did they see? They saw a group of men on horseback, in military dress; but the foremost man, on whom all eyes were bent, was a tall, splendid figure, erect upon his horse; those nearest could see that he had a rosy face, thick brown hair that was brushed back from his face, and clear blue eyes set rather far apart. By his side was a man who appeared even taller, he was so thin and lank; he had a huge nose, eyes that were looking in every direction, and a mouth that seemed almost ready to laugh at the people before him. He sat easily and carelessly on his horse. This was General Lee.

Now, the strong Virginian, easily marked by his bearing and his striking dress, — for he wore a blue coat with buff facings, buff small-clothes, an epaulet on each shoulder, and a cockade in his hat, — turned to General Ward, who had heretofore been in command of the army, and laying his hand on the hilt of his sword, drew it from the scabbard, and raised it in the sight of the people. The cannon roared, no doubt, and the people shouted. It was a great occasion for them, and everybody was on tiptoe to see the Virginians. All this is what we may suppose, for there is no account of the exact ceremony. We only know that, at that time, Washington took command of the army.

But what did Washington see, and what did he think, now, and later, when he made a tour of inspection through the camp and to the outposts? He saw a motley assembly, in all sorts of uniforms and without any uniform at all, with all sorts of weapons and with precious little powder. So little was there that Washington was very anxious lest the British should find out how little he had; and so while he was urging Congress to provide supplies, he had barrels of sand, with powder covering the top, placed in the magazine, that any spy hanging about might be misled. Some of the soldiers were in tents, some were quartered in one or two college buildings then standing, and some built huts for themselves. The most orderly camp was that of the Rhode Island troops, under General Nathanael Greene.

The men were in companies of various sizes, under captains and other officers who had very little authority over the privates, for these usually elected their own commanders. A visitor to the camp relates a dialogue which he heard between a captain and one of the privates under him.

"Bill," said the captain, "go and bring a pail of water for the men."

"I sha'n't," said Bill. "It's your turn now, Captain; I got it last time."

But the men, though under very little discipline, were good stuff out of which to make soldiers. Most of them were in dead earnest, and they brought, besides courage, great skill in the use of the ordinary musket. A story is told of a company of riflemen raised in one of the frontier counties of Pennsylvania. So many volunteers applied as to embarrass the leader who was enlisting the company, and he drew on a board with chalk the figure of a nose of the common size, placed the board at the distance of a hundred and fifty yards, and then declared he would take only those who could hit the mark. Over sixty succeeded. "General Gage, take care of *your* nose," says the newspaper that tells the story. General Gage, as you know, was the commander of the British forces in Boston.

Washington wrote to Congress, "I have a sincere pleasure in observing that there are materials for a good army, a great number of able-bodied men, active, zealous in the cause, and of unquestionable courage."

His first business was to make an army out of this material, and he shrewdly suggested that inasmuch as there was great need of clothing, it would be well to furnish ten thousand hunting-shirts at once. Not only would these be the cheapest garments, but they would furnish a convenient and characteristic uniform, which would destroy the distinctions between the troops from different colonies or towns. If the men looked alike, they would act together better.

There is a story that Washington had a platform built in the branches of the elm under which he had taken command of the army, and that there he sat with his glass, spying the movements across the water in Boston. Whether this be so or not, he was constantly scouring the country himself, and sending his scouts within the enemy's lines. The most critical time came at the end of the year 1775, when the term of the old soldiers' enlistment expired, and the ranks were filling up with raw recruits.

"It is not in the pages of history, perhaps," writes Washington to the president of Congress, on the 4th of January, "to furnish a case like ours. To maintain a post within musket-shot of the enemy for six months together without and at the same time to disband one army and recruit another, within that distance of twenty odd British regiments, is more, probably, than ever was attempted. But if we succeed as well in the last as we have heretofore in the first, I shall think it the most fortunate event of my whole life."

The blank purposely left in this letter, in case it should fall into the hands of the enemy, was easily filled by Congress with the word "powder."

At one time there was not half a pound to a man. General Sullivan writes that when General Washington heard of this, he was so much struck by the danger that he did not utter a word for half an hour.

When Washington left Philadelphia for Cambridge, he wrote to his wife as if he expected to return after a short campaign. Perhaps he said this to comfort her. Perhaps he really hoped that by a short, sharp struggle the colonies would show Great Britain that they were in earnest, and would secure the rights which had been taken from them. At any rate, from the day he took command of the army in Cambridge, Washington had one purpose in view, to attack Boston just as soon as possible. The summer was not over before he called his officers together and proposed to make the attack. They hesitated, and finally said they were not ready for so bold a move. He called a council again, the middle of October, but still he could not bring them to the point. He kept on urging it, however, as the one thing to do, and Congress at last, just at the end of the year, passed a resolution giving Washington authority to make an assault upon the British forces " in any manner he might think expedient, notwithstanding the town and property in it might be destroyed."

As soon as he received this authority, Washington again called his officers together, and urged with all his might the necessity of immediate action. He thought they should make a bold attempt at once to conquer the English army in Boston. In the spring more troops would come over from England. "Strike now!" he said, "and perhaps it will not be necessary to strike again." But it was not till the middle of February that he was able to persuade his generals to agree to a move. As soon as he had won them over, he made his preparations as rapidly as possible, and on the 3d of March took possession of Dorchester Heights. That movement showed the British what was coming. If they were to stay in Boston, they would at once be attacked. They took to their ships and sailed out of Boston harbor.

Washington had driven them out, though he had fought no battle. It is impossible to say what would have happened if he could have had his way before, and attacked Boston. There were many friends of America in Parliament, and if the news had come that the New England men had actually destroyed Boston, the town where their property was, in their determination to drive out the British soldiers, I think these friends would have said: "See how much in earnest these Massachusetts men are! They have a right to be heard, when they are willing to sacrifice their own town to secure their rights." Boston was not destroyed, and the war went on; but one effect of this siege of Boston was to inspire confidence in Washington. He showed that he was a born leader. He did not hold back, but went right to the front, and beckoned to the other generals to come and stand where he stood. He had courage; he was ready to attack the enemy. It was a righteous cause in which he was embarked, and he wished to make short work of the business. There were to be seven weary years of war, and Washington was to show in other ways that he was the leader; but it was a great thing that in the beginning of the struggle he should have been head and shoulders above the men around him, and that when he drew his sword from the scabbard he was no boaster, but was ready at once to use it.

CHAPTER XVI.

LEADING THE ARMY.

On the 13th of April, 1776, Washington was in New York, which now promised to be the centre of operations. Here he remained four or five months, making one visit meanwhile to Philadelphia, at the request of Congress, which wished to confer with him. He was busy increasing and strengthening the army and erecting fortifications.

That spring and summer saw a rapid change in men's minds regarding the war with England. Washington no longer thought it possible to obtain what the colonies demanded and still remain subject to England. He was ready for independence, and when Congress issued its declaration, Washington had it read before the army with great satisfaction.

Not long after the Declaration of Independence an English fleet arrived in New York Bay, bringing a large body of troops, under the command of Lord Howe, who, with his brother Admiral Howe, had been appointed commissioners to treat with the Americans. In reality, they only brought a promise of pardon to the rebels. It was very clear to Washington that the British government had not the slightest intention of listening to the grievances of the colonies with a desire to redress them; but that they meant by these proposals to distract the colonies, if possible, and build up a party there that would oppose the action of Congress. There was a little incident attending the arrival of the commissioners that showed the feeling which prevailed.

One afternoon, word came that a boat was coming to headquarters, bringing a messenger from Lord Howe with a communication. Washington had noticed that the British, whenever speaking of him or other American officers, had refused to regard them as officers of the army; they were simply private gentlemen who had taken up arms against the king. Now Washington knew that while it was in itself a small matter whether he was addressed by people about him as General Washington or Mr. Washington, it was not at all a small matter how Lord Howe addressed him. That officer had no business with George Washington, but he might have very important business with General Washington. Accordingly, he called together such of the American officers as were at headquarters to consult them in regard to the subject, and they agreed entirely with him. Colonel Reed was directed to receive the messenger and manage the matter.

Accordingly, he entered a boat and was rowed out toward Staten Island, whence Lord Howe's messenger was coming. The two boats met halfway, and Lieutenant Brown — for that was the name of the messenger — was very polite, and informed Colonel Reed that he bore a letter from General Howe to Mr. Washington. Colonel Reed looked surprised. He himself was an officer in the Continental army, and he knew no such person. Thereupon Lieutenant Brown showed him the letter, which was addressed, George Washington, Esq. Colonel Reed was polite, but it was quite impossible for him to bear a letter to the commander of the American army addressed in that way. The lieutenant was embarrassed; as a gentleman and an officer he saw he was in the wrong. He tried to make matters better by saying that it was an important letter, but was intended rather for a person who was of great importance in American councils than for one who was commanding an army.

Colonel Reed continued to refuse the letter, and the boats parted. Presently, however, Lieutenant Brown came rowing back and asked by what title Washington chose to be addressed. It was quite an unnecessary question, Reed thought. There was not the slightest doubt as to what General Washington's rank was. The lieutenant knew it and was really very sorry, but he wished Colonel Reed would take the letter. Colonel Reed replied that it was the easiest matter in the world; it only needed that the letter should be correctly addressed. And so they parted.

Five days later, an aide-de-camp of General Howe appeared with a flag and asked that an interview might be granted to Colonel Patterson, the British Adjutant-General. Consent was given, and the next day Washington, with all his officers about him, received Colonel Patterson, who was very polite, and addressed him as "Your Excellency," which did quite well, though it was dodging matters somewhat. He tried to explain away the affair of the letter, and said that no impertinence was intended, and he then produced another, addressed to George Washington, Esq., etc., etc.

Evidently, Lord Howe thought he had invented a capital way out of the difficulty. *Et cetera, et cetera!* Why, that might cover everything, — General-Commanding, Lord High Rebel, or anything else this very punctilious Virginia gentleman might fancy as his title. It would save Washington's pride and relieve Lord Howe's scruples. Washington replied coolly, Yes, the *et cetera* implied everything, but it also implied anything or nothing. It was meaningless. He was not a private person; this letter was meant for a public character, and as such he could not receive it, unless it acknowledged him properly. So Colonel Patterson was obliged to pocket the letter, and try to cover his mortification and to deliver the contents verbally.

Perhaps all this sounds like very small business. In reality it meant a great deal. Were Washington and other officers rebels against the king, or were they the officers of a government which declared itself independent of the king? Lord Howe gave up trying to force Washington into the trap, and wrote to his government that it would be necessary in future to give the American commander his title; and Congress, to whom Washington reported the matter, passed a resolution approving of his course, and directing that no letter or message be received on any occasion whatsoever from the enemy, by the commander-in-chief or by other commanders of the American army, but such as should be directed to them in the characters they respectively sustained. Little things like this went a great way toward making the people stand erect and look the world in the face.

The Americans needed, indeed, all the aid and comfort they could get, for it was plain that they were at a great disadvantage, with their half-equipped troops stationed some on Long Island and some in New York, between the North and East rivers, surrounded by Tories, who took courage from the presence of a large British force in the bay. Washington used his best endeavors to bring about a strong spirit of patriotism in the camp which should put an end to petty sectional jealousies, and he felt the sacredness of the cause in which they were engaged so deeply that he could not bear to have the army act or think otherwise than as the servants of God. He issued a general order, which ran as follows: —

"That the troops may have an opportunity of attending public worship, as well as to take some rest after the great fatigue they have gone through, the general, in future, excuses them from fatigue duty on Sundays, except at the ship-yards, or on special occasions, until further orders. The general is sorry to be informed that the foolish and wicked practice of profane cursing and swearing, — a vice heretofore little known in an American army, — is growing into fashion; he hopes the officers will, by example as well as influence, endeavor to check it, and that both they and the men will reflect, that we can have little hope of the blessing of Heaven on our arms, if we insult it by our impiety and folly; added to this, it is a vice so mean and low, without any temptation, that every man of sense and character detests and despises it."

The time was now at hand when the army would be put to a severe test, and Washington was to show his generalship in other and more striking ways. The battle of Long Island was fought August 27, 1776, and was a severe blow to the American army. Washington's first business was to withdraw such of the forces as remained on Long Island to the mainland, and unite the two parts of his army. He had nine thousand men and their baggage and arms to bring across a swift strait, while a victorious enemy was so near that their movements could be plainly heard.

Now his skill and energy were seen. He sent verbal orders for all the boats of whatever size that lay along the New York shore up the Hudson and on the East River to be brought to the Brooklyn side. He issued orders for the troops to hold themselves in readiness to attack the enemy at night, and he made the troops that defended the outer line of breastworks to have all the air of preparation as if they were about to move at once upon the enemy. All this time it was raining and uncomfortable enough, for the soldiers were unprotected by tents or shelter of any kind, save such rude barriers as they could raise. They kept up a brisk firing at the outposts, and the men who held the advanced position were on the alert, expecting every moment orders to advance.

Then they heard dull sounds in the distance toward the water. Suddenly at about two o'clock in the morning a cannon went off with a tremendous explosion. Nobody knew what it was, and to this day the accident remains a mystery. But the soldiers discovered what was going on. A retreat instead of an advance had been ordered. The order for an advance was intended to conceal the plan. Washington was on the shore superintending the embarkation of the troops. Some had gone over; when the tide turned, the wind and current were against them; there were not enough boats to carry the rest. To add to the confusion one of the officers blundered, and the men who had been kept in front to conceal the movement from the British were ordered down to the Ferry. For a while it looked as if the retreat would be discovered, but it was not, and when morning came the entire army had been moved across to New York, and not a man in the British army knew what had been done. It was a great feat, and Washington, who had not closed his eyes for forty-eight hours, and scarcely left the saddle all that time, again showed himself a masterly general.

He had now to show the same kind of ability the rest of the autumn. It requires one kind of generalship to lead men into battle and another to lead them on a retreat away from the enemy. With a large fleet in the harbor, it was clear that the British could at any time destroy New York and any army that was there. Accordingly, Washington withdrew his army up the island. The British followed. They could transport troops on both sides of the island, by water, and could prevent the Americans from crossing the Hudson River into New Jersey. They began to land troops on the shore of East River not far from where is now the Thirty-fourth Street Ferry. Some breastworks had been thrown up there, and were held by soldiers who had been in the battle of Long Island. They seem to have been thoroughly demoralized by that defeat, for they fled as soon as they saw the British advancing, and other troops which had been sent to reinforce them were also seized with panic and fled.

Washington heard the firing in this direction and galloped over to the scene. He met the soldiers running away and called on them to halt. But they were overcome by fear and had lost their self-command. They paid no heed to him, and Washington, usually cool and self-possessed, was so enraged by their cowardly behavior that he flew into a transport of rage, flung down his hat, exclaiming, "Are these the men with whom I am to defend America!" and drawing his pistols and sword in turn, rushed upon the fugitives, trying to drive them back to their duty. He had no fear of danger himself, and was within a short distance of the British, riding about furiously, when one of his aids, seeing the danger, seized the horse's bridle and called his commander to his senses.

To cover the army, Washington posted his forces across the narrow upper part of the island, from Fort Washington on the Hudson to the Harlem River, and here he kept the British at bay while his men recovered their strength and were ready for further movements. Meanwhile, across the Hudson River from Fort Washington, another fort, named from General Lee, had been built, and Washington had posted General Greene there. It was evident that with the British in force, with an army and navy, it would be impossible to hold New York or the Hudson River, and it was also clear that should Washington's army be defeated there, the British would at once move on Philadelphia, where Congress was sitting. With New York commanding the Hudson River, and with Philadelphia in their hands, the British would have control of the most important parts of America.

Washington saw also that there was hard work before him, and that it would be impossible to carry on the war with an army which was enlisted for a year only, and he bent his energies toward persuading Congress to enlist men for a longer period. He had to organize this new army and to superintend countless details. His old habits of method and accuracy stood him in good stead now, and he worked incessantly, getting affairs into order, for he knew that the British would soon move. Indeed, it is one of the strange things in history that the British, with the immense advantage which they had, did not at once after the battle of Long Island press forward and break down the Continental army in a quick succession of attacks by land and water. It is quite certain that Washington, in their place, would not have delayed action.

At the end of October, Washington occupied a position at White Plains, in the rocky, hilly country north of New York. Step by step he had given way before General Howe, who had been trying to get the American army where he could surround it and destroy it. Washington, on the other hand, could not afford to run any risks. He wished to delay the British as long as possible, and not fight them till he had his new army well organized. There was a battle at White Plains, and the Americans were forced back; but Washington suddenly changed his position, moved his men quickly to a stronger place, and began to dig intrenchments. He was too weak to fight in the open field, but he could fight with his spade, and he meant to give Howe all the trouble he could. He expected another attack, but in a day or two there were signs of a movement, and he discovered that the enemy was leaving his front.

He was not quite certain what Howe's plans might be, but he was quite sure he would move on Philadelphia. Meanwhile, he kept watch over Fort Washington, and gave orders that it should be held only so long as it was prudent, but that in case of extreme danger, it should be given up and its garrison cross the river to Fort Lee. He himself, with all but the New England troops, crossed the river higher up, at King's Ferry. The New England and New York troops he posted on both sides of the river to defend the passes in the Highlands, for it was of great importance to have open communication between Philadelphia and New England. A division also was left under

General Lee at White Plains, who was to be ready to join Washington when it should become necessary.

General Greene, who was in command at Fort Lee, on the New Jersey side of the Hudson, hoped to keep Fort Washington, on the New York side, which was also under his command. He hoped to keep it even after the British had begun to lay siege to it. Washington was obliged to leave this business to Greene's discretion, for he was occupied with moving his army across the river, higher up, and if the fort could have held out, they might have been able to prevent the British from crossing to New Jersey. But Greene counted on a stouter defense than the men in the fort gave, and when Washington at last reached Fort Lee it was only to see from the banks of the river the surrender of Fort Washington with its military stores and two thousand men. It was a terrible loss; and, moreover, the capture of that fort made it impossible to hold Fort Lee, which was at once abandoned.

Now began a wonderful retreat. The English under Lord Cornwallis, with a well-equipped army, and flushed with recent victory, crossed over to New Jersey and began moving forward. They were so prompt that the Americans left their kettles on the fire in Fort Lee as they hastily left. Washington, with a small, ragged, discouraged army, fell back from the enemy, sometimes leaving a town at one end as the British entered it at the other; but he broke down bridges, he destroyed provisions, and so hampered and delayed the enemy that they made less than seventy miles over level country in nineteen days.

Meanwhile the British general was issuing proclamations calling upon the people of New Jersey to return to their allegiance, and promising them pardon. Many gave up and asked protection. It seemed as if the war were coming to an end, and that all the struggle had been in vain. The American army, moreover, had been enlisted for a short term only, and before the end of December most of the men would have served their time. General Lee delayed and delayed, and Washington himself was harassed and well-nigh disheartened; but he meant to die hard. One day, when affairs looked very dark, he turned to Colonel Reed, who was by him, and said, drawing his hand significantly across his throat: "Reed, my neck does not feel as though it was made for a halter. We must retire to Augusta County in Virginia, and if overpowered, must pass the Alleghany Mountains."

But Washington was made for something more than a guerrilla chieftain. He had put the Delaware River between his army and the British, who were now scattered over New Jersey, going into winter quarters, and intending, when the river was frozen, to cross on the ice and move upon

WASHINGTON CROSSING THE DELAWARE.

Philadelphia. Suddenly, on Christmas night, Washington recrossed the river with his little army, making a perilous passage through cakes of floating ice that crunched against the boats, surprised a large detachment of Hessians near Trenton, and captured a thousand prisoners. Eight days later he fought the battle of Princeton. Within three weeks he had completely turned the tables. He had driven the enemy from every post it occupied in New Jersey, except Brunswick and Amboy, made Philadelphia safe, and shown the people that the army, which was thought to be on the verge of destruction, could be used in the hands of a great general like a rod with which to punish the enemy.

Men were beginning to see that here was one who was a true leader of men.

On the day after the victory at Trenton, Congress, "having maturely considered the present crisis, and having perfect reliance on the wisdom, vigor, and uprightness of General Washington," passed a resolution that "General Washington shall be, and he is hereby, vested with full, ample, and complete powers to raise armies, appoint officers, and exercise control over the parts of the country occupied by the army." Washington had been constantly checked by the necessity of referring all questions to Congress and to his generals. Now he was to have full power, for he had shown himself a man fit to be trusted with power.

CHAPTER XVII.

AT VALLEY FORGE.

THE winter of 1777 passed with little fighting; and when the spring opened, Washington used his army so adroitly as to prevent the British from moving on Philadelphia, and finally crowded them out of New Jersey altogether. That summer, however, was an anxious one, for there was great uncertainty as to the plans of the enemy; and when at last a formidable British army appeared in the Chesapeake, whither it had been transported by sea, Washington hurried his forces to meet it, and fought the battle of Brandywine, in which he met with a severe loss. He retrieved his fortune in part by a brilliant attack on the enemy at Germantown, and then retired to Valley Forge, in Pennsylvania, where he went into winter quarters; while the British army was comfortably established in Philadelphia.

The defeat of Burgoyne by Gates, at Saratoga, in the summer and Washington's splendid attack at Germantown had made a profound impression in Europe, and are counted as having turned the scale in favor of an alliance with the United States on the part of France. But when the winter shut

AT VALLEY FORGE. 171

down on the American army, no such good cheer encouraged it. That winter of 1778 was the most terrible ordeal which the army endured, and one has but to read of the sufferings of the soldiers to learn at how great a cost independence was bought. It is worth while to tell again the familiar story, because the leader of the army himself shared the want and privation of the men. To read of Valley Forge is to read of Washington.

The place was chosen for winter quarters because of its position. It was equally distant with Philadelphia from the Brandywine and from the ferry across the Delaware into New Jersey. It was too far from Philadelphia to be in peril from attack, and yet it was so near that the American army could, if opportunity offered, descend quickly on the city. Then it was so protected by hills and streams that the addition of a few lines of fortification made it very secure.

But there was no town at Valley Forge, and it became necessary to provide some shelter for the soldiers other than the canvas tents which served in the field in summer. It was the middle of December when the army began preparations for the winter, and Washington gave directions for the building of the little village. The men were divided into parties of twelve, each party to build a hut to accommodate that number; and in order to stimulate the men, Washington promised a reward of twelve dollars to the party in each regiment which finished its hut first and most satisfactorily. And as there was some difficulty in getting boards, he offered a hundred dollars to any officer or soldier who should invent some substitute which would be as cheap as boards and as quickly provided.

Each hut was to be fourteen feet by sixteen, the sides, ends, and roof to be made of logs, and the sides made tight with clay. There was to be a fireplace in the rear of each hut, built of wood, but lined with clay eighteen inches thick. The walls were to be six and a half feet high. Huts were also to be provided for the officers, and to be placed in the rear of those occupied by the troops. All these were to be regularly arranged in streets. A visitor to the camp when the huts were being built wrote of the army: "They appear to me like a family of beavers, every one busy; some carrying logs, others mud, and the rest plastering them together." It was bitterly cold, and for a month the men were at work, making ready for the winter.

But in what sort of condition were the men themselves when they began this work? Here is a picture of one of those men on his way to Valley Forge: "His bare feet peep through his worn-out shoes, his legs nearly naked from the tattered remains of an only pair of stockings, his breeches not enough to cover his nakedness, his shirt hanging in strings, his hair disheveled, his face wan and thin, his look hungry, his whole appearance that of a man forsaken and neglected." And the snow was falling! This was one of the privates. The officers were scarcely better off. One was wrapped "in a sort of dressing-gown made of an old blanket or woolen bed-cover." The uniforms were torn and ragged; the guns were rusty; a few only had bayonets; the soldiers carried their powder in tin boxes and cow-horns.

To explain why this army was so poor and forlorn would be to tell a long story. It may be summed up briefly in these words: The army was not taken care of because there was no country to take care of it. There were thirteen States, and each of these States sent troops into the field, but all the States were jealous of one another. There was a Congress, which undertook to direct the war, but all the members of Congress, coming from the several States, were jealous of one another. They were agreed on only one thing — that it was not prudent to give the army too much power. It is true that they had once given Washington large authority, but they had given it only for a short period. They were very much afraid that somehow the army would rule the country, and yet they were trying to free the country from the rule of England. But when they talked about freeing the country, each man thought only of his own State. The first fervor with which they had talked about a common country had died away;

there were some very selfish men in Congress, who could not be patriotic enough to think of the whole country.

The truth is, it takes a long time for the people of a country to come to feel that they have a country. Up to the time of the war for independence, the people in America did not care much for one another or for America. They had really been preparing to be a nation, but they did not know it. They were angry with Great Britain, and they knew they had been wronged. They were therefore ready to fight; but it does not require so much courage to fight as to endure suffering and to be patient.

So it was that the people of America who were most conscious that they were Americans were the men who were in the army, and their wives and mothers and sisters at home. All these were making sacrifices for their country and so learning to love it. The men in the army came from different States, and there was a great deal of state feeling among them; but, after all, they belonged to one army, — the Continental army, — and they had much more in common than they had separately. Especially they had a great leader who made no distinction between Virginians and New England men. Washington felt keenly all the lack of confidence which Congress showed. He saw that the spirit in Congress was one which kept the people divided, while the spirit at Valley Forge kept the people united, and he wrote reproachfully to Congress: —

"If we would pursue a right system of policy, in my opinion, . . . we should all, Congress and army, be considered as one people, embarked in one cause, in one interest; acting on the same principle, and to the same end. The distinction, the jealousies set up or perhaps only incautiously let out, can answer not a single good purpose. . . . No order of men in the thirteen States has paid a more sacred regard to the proceedings of Congress than the army; for without arrogance or the smallest deviation from truth, it may be said that no history now extant can furnish an instance of an army's suffering such uncommon hardships as ours has done, and bearing them with the same patience and fortitude. To see men, without clothes to cover them, without blankets to lie on, without shoes (for the want of which their marches might be traced by the blood from their feet), and almost as often without provisions as with them, marching through the frost and snow, and at Christmas taking up their winter quarters within a day's march of the enemy, without a house or hut to cover them, till they could be built, and submitting without a murmur, is a proof of patience and obedience, which, in my opinion, can scarce be paralleled."

The horses died of starvation, and the men harnessed themselves to trucks and sleds, hauling wood and provisions from storehouse to hut. At one time there was not a ration in camp. Washington seized the peril with a strong hand and compelled the people in the country about, who had been selling to the British army at Philadelphia, to give up their stores to the patriots at Valley Forge.

Meanwhile, the wives of the officers came to the camp, and these brave women gave of their cheer to its dreary life. Mrs. Washington was there with her husband. "The general's apartment is very small," she wrote to a friend; "he has had a log cabin built to dine in, which has made our quarters much more tolerable than they were at first."

The officers and their wives came together and told stories, perhaps over a plate of hickory nuts, which, we are informed, furnished General Washington's dessert. The general was cheerful in the little society; but his one thought was how to keep the brave company of men alive and prepare them for what lay before them. The house where he had his quarters was a farm-house belonging to a Quaker, Mr. Potts, who has said that one day when strolling up the creek, away from the camp, he heard a deep, quiet voice a little way off. He went nearer, and saw Washington's horse tied to a sapling. Hard by, in the thicket, was Washington on his knees, praying earnestly.

At the end of February, light began to break. The terrible winter was passing away, though the army was still in a wretched state. But there came to camp a volunteer, Baron Steuben, who had been trained in the best armies of Europe. In him Washington had, what he greatly needed, an excellent drill-master. He made him Inspector of the army, and soon, as if by magic, the men changed from slouching, careless fellows into erect, orderly soldiers. The baron began with a picked company of one hundred and twenty men, whom he drilled thoroughly; these became the models for others, and so the whole camp was turned into a military school.

The prospect grew brighter and brighter, until on the 4th of May, late at night, a messenger rode into camp with despatches from Congress. Washington opened them, and his heart must have leaped for joy as he read that an alliance had been formed between France and the United States. Two days later, the army celebrated the event. The chaplains of the several regiments read the intelligence and then offered up thanksgiving to God. Guns were fired, and there was a public dinner in honor of Washington and his generals. There had been shouts for the king of France and for the American States; but when Washington took his leave, "there was," says an officer who was present, universal applause, " with loud huzzas, which continued till he had proceeded a quarter of a mile, during which time there were a thousand hats tossed in the air. His excellency turned round with his retinue, and huzzaed several times."

CHAPTER XVIII.

THE CONWAY CABAL.

THERE is no man so high but some will always be found who wish to pull him down. Washington was no exception to this rule. His men worshiped him; the people had confidence in him; the officers nearest to him, and especially those who formed a part of his military family, were warmly attached to him; but in Congress there were men who violently opposed him, and there were certain generals who not only envied him but were ready to seize any opportunity which might offer to belittle him and to place one of their own number in his place. The chief men who were engaged in this business were Generals Conway, Mifflin, and Gates, and from the prominent position taken in the affair by the first-named officer, the intrigue against Washington goes by the name of the Conway Cabal. A "cabal" is a secret combination against a person with the object of his hurt or injury.

It is not easy to say just how or when this cabal first showed itself. Conway was a young brigadier-general, very conceited and impudent. Mifflin had been quartermaster-general, but had resigned. He had been early in the service, and was in Cambridge with Washington, but had long been secretly hostile to him. Gates, who had been Washington's companion in Virginia, was an ambitious man who never lost an opportunity of looking after his own interest, and had been especially fortunate in being appointed to the command of the northern army just as it achieved the famous victory over Burgoyne.

The defeat at Brandywine, the failure to make Germantown a great success, and the occupation of Philadelphia by the British troops, while the American army was suffering at Valley Forge — all this seemed to many a sorry story compared with the brilliant victory at Saratoga. There had always been those who thought Washington slow and cautious. John Adams was one of these, and he expressed himself as heartily glad "that the glory of turning the tide of arms was not immediately due to the commander-in-chief." Others shook their heads and said that the people of America had been guilty of idolatry by making a man their god; and that, besides, the army would become dangerous to the liberties of the people if it were allowed to be so influenced by one man.

Conway was the foremost of these critics. "No man was more a gentleman than General Washington, or appeared to more advantage at his table, or in the usual intercourse of life," he would say; then he would give his shoulders a shrug, and look around and add, "but as to his talents for the command of an army, they were miserable indeed."

"Gates was the general!" Conway said. "There was a man who could fight, and win victories!"

Gates himself was in a mood to believe it. He had been so intoxicated by his success against Burgoyne that he thought himself the man of the day, and quite forgot to send a report of the action to his commander-in-chief. Washington rebuked him in a letter which was severe in its quiet tone. He congratulated Gates on his great success, and added, "At the same time, I cannot but regret that a matter of such magnitude, and so interesting to our general operations, should have reached me by report only; or through the channel of letters not bearing that authenticity which the importance of it required, and which it would have received by a line over your signature stating the simple fact."

Gates may have winced under the rebuke, but he was then listening to Conway's flattery, and that was more agreeable to him. Conway, on his part, found Gates a convenient man to set up as a rival to Washington. He himself did not aspire to be commander-in-chief, though he would have had no doubt as to his capacity. Washington knew him well. "His merit as an officer," wrote the commander-in-chief, "and his importance in this army exist more in his own imagination than in reality. For it is a maxim with him to leave no service of his untold, nor to want anything which is to be obtained by importunity." Conway thought Gates was the rising man, and he meant to rise with him. He filled his ear with things which he thought would please him, and among other letters wrote him one in which these words occurred: " Heaven has determined to save your country, or a weak general and bad counselors would have ruined it."

Now Gates was foolish enough to show this letter to Wilkinson, one of his aids, and Wilkinson repeated it to an aid of Lord Stirling, one of Washington's generals, and Lord Stirling at once sat down and wrote it off to Washington. Thereupon Washington, who knew Conway too well to waste any words upon him, sat down and wrote him this letter: —

"SIR, — A letter which I received last night contained the following paragraph: —

"'In a letter from General Conway to General Gates he says: Heaven has determined to save your country, or a weak general and bad counselors would have ruined it.'

"I am, Sir, your humble servant,

"GEORGE WASHINGTON."

That was all, but it was quite enough to throw Conway and Gates and Mifflin into a panic. How did Washington get hold of the sentence? Had he seen any other letters? How much did he know? In point of fact, that was all that Washington had seen. He had a contempt for Conway. He knew of Mifflin's hostility and that Gates was now cool to him; but he did not suspect Gates of any intrigue, and he supposed for a while that Wilkinson's message had been intended only to warn him of Conway's evil mind.

Gates was greatly perplexed to know what to do, but he finally wrote to Washington as if there were some wretch who had been stealing letters and might be discovering the secrets of the American leaders. He begged Washington to help him find the rascal. Washington replied, giving him the exact manner in which the letter came into his hands, and then closed with a few sentences that showed Gates clearly that he had lost the confidence of his commander-in-chief.

That particular occasion passed; but presently the cabal showed its head again, this time working through Congress. It secured the appointment of a Board of War, with Gates at the head, and a majority of the members from men who were hostile to Washington. Now, they thought, Washington will resign, and to help matters on they spread the report that Washington was about to resign. The general checkmated them at once by a letter to a friend, in which he wrote: —

"To report a design of this kind is among the arts

which those who are endeavoring to effect a change are practicing to bring it to pass. . . . While the public are satisfied with my endeavors, I mean not to shrink from the cause. But the moment her voice, *not that of faction,* calls upon me to resign, I shall do it with as much pleasure as ever the wearied traveler retired to rest."

The cabal was not yet defeated. It had failed by roundabout methods. It looked about in Congress and counted the disaffected to see if it would be possible to get a majority vote in favor of a motion to arrest the commander-in-chief. So at least the story runs which, from its nature, would not be found in any record, but was whispered from one man to another. The day came when the motion was to be tried; the conspiracy leaked out, and Washington's friends bestirred themselves. They needed one more vote. They sent post-haste for one of their number, Gouverneur Morris, who was absent in camp; but they feared they could not get him in time. In their extremity, they went to William Duer, a member from New York, who was dangerously ill. Duer sent for his doctor.

"Doctor," he asked, "can I be carried to Congress?"

"Yes, but at the risk of your life," replied the physician.

"Do you mean that I should expire before reaching the place?" earnestly inquired the patient.

"No," came the answer; "but I would not answer for your leaving it alive."

"Very well, sir. You have done your duty and I will do mine!" exclaimed Duer. "Prepare a litter for me; if you will not, somebody else will, but I prefer your aid."

The demand was in earnest, and Duer had already started when it was announced that Morris had returned and that he would not be needed. Morris had come direct from the camp with the latest news of what was going on there. His vote would make it impossible for the enemies of Washington to carry their point; their opportunity was lost, and they never recovered it.

It was not the end of the cabal, however. They still cherished their hostility to Washington, and they sought to injure him where he would feel the wound most keenly. They tried to win from him the young Marquis de La Fayette, who had come from France to join the American army, and whom Washington had taken to his heart. La Fayette was ambitious and enthusiastic. Conway, who had been in France, did his best to attach himself to the young Frenchman, but he betrayed his hatred of Washington, and that was enough to estrange La Fayette. Then a winter campaign in Canada was planned, and the cabal intrigued to have La Fayette appointed to command it. It was argued that as a Frenchman he would have an influence over the French Canadians. But the plotters hoped that, away from Washington, the young marquis could be more easily worked upon, and it was intended that Conway should be his second in command.

Of course, in contriving this plan, Washington was not consulted; but the moment La Fayette was approached, he appealed to Washington for advice. Washington saw through the device, but he at once said, "I would rather it should be you than another." La Fayette insisted on Kalb being second in command instead of Conway, whom he disliked and distrusted. Congress was in session at York, and thither La Fayette went to receive his orders. Gates, who spent much of his time in the neighborhood of Congress, seeking to influence the members, was there, and La Fayette was at once invited to join him and his friends at dinner. The talk ran freely, and great things were promised of the Canada expedition, but not a word was said about Washington. La Fayette listened and noticed. He thought of the contrast between the meagre fare and the sacrifices at Valley Forge, and this feast at which he was a guest. He watched his opportunity, and near the end of the dinner, he said: —

"I have a toast to propose. There is one health, gentlemen, which we have not yet drunk. I have the honor to propose it to you: The commander-in-chief of the armies of the United States!"

It was a challenge which no one dared openly

to take up, but there was an end to the good spirits of the company. La Fayette had shown his colors, and he was let alone after that. Indeed, the Canada expedition never was undertaken, for the men who were urging it were not in earnest about anything but diminishing the honor of Washington. It is the nature of cabals and intrigues that they flourish in the dark. They cannot bear the light. As soon as these hostile intentions began to reach the ears of the public, great was the indignation aroused, and one after another of the conspirators made haste to disown any evil purpose. Gates and Mifflin each publicly avowed their entire confidence in Washington, and Conway, who had fought a duel and supposed himself to be dying, made a humble apology. The cabal melted away, leaving Washington more secure than ever in the confidence of men — all the more secure that he did not lower himself by attempting the same arts against his traducers. When Conway was uttering his libels behind his back, Washington was openly declaring his judgment of Conway; and throughout the whole affair, Washington kept his hands clean, and went his way with a manly disregard of his enemies.

CHAPTER XIX.

MONMOUTH.

THE news of the French alliance, and consequent war between France and England, compelled the English to leave Philadelphia. They had taken their ease there during the winter, while hardships and Steuben's drilling and Washington's unflagging zeal had made the American army at Valley Forge strong and determined. A French fleet might at any time sail up the Delaware, and with the American army in the rear, Philadelphia would be a hard place to hold. So General Howe turned his command over to General Clinton, and went home to England, and General Clinton set about marching his army across New Jersey to New York.

The moment the troops left Philadelphia armed men sprang up all over New Jersey to contest their passage, and Washington set his army in motion, following close upon the heels of the enemy, who were making for Staten Island. There was a question whether they should attack the British and bring on a general engagement, or only follow them and vex them. The generals on whom Washington most relied, Greene, La Fayette, and Wayne, all good fighters, urged that it would be a shame to let the enemy leave New Jersey without a severe punishment. The majority of generals in the council, however, strongly opposed the plan of giving battle. They said that the French alliance would undoubtedly put an end to the war at once. Why, then, risk life and success? The British army, moreover, was strong and well equipped.

The most strenuous opponent of the fighting plan was General Charles Lee. When he was left in command of a body of troops at the time of Washington's crossing the Hudson River more than a year before, his orders were to hold himself in readiness to join Washington at any time. In his march across New Jersey, Washington had repeatedly sent for Lee, but Lee had delayed in an unaccountable manner, and finally was himself surprised by a company of dragoons, and taken captive. For a year he had been held a prisoner, and only lately had been released on exchange. He had returned to the army while the cabal against Washington was going on, and had taken part in it, for he always felt that he ought to be first and Washington second. He was second in command now, and his opinion had great weight. He was a trained soldier, and besides, in his long captivity he had become well acquainted with General Clinton, and he professed to know well the condition and temper of the British officers.

Washington thus found himself unsupported by a majority of his officers. But he had no doubt in his own mind that the policy of attack was a sound one. All had agreed that it was well to harass the enemy; he therefore ordered La Fayette with a large division to fall upon the enemy at an exposed point. He thought it not unlikely that this would bring on a general action, and he disposed his forces so as to be ready for such an emergency. He gave the command to La Fayette, because Lee had disapproved the plan; but after La Fayette had set out, Lee came to Washington and declared that La Fayette's division was so large as to make it almost an independent army, and that therefore he would like to change his mind and take command. It never would do to have his junior in such authority.

Here was a dilemma. Washington could not recall La Fayette. He wished to make use of Lee; so he gave Lee two additional brigades, sent him forward to join La Fayette, when, as his senior, he would of course command the entire force; and at the same time he notified La Fayette of what he had done, trusting to his sincere devotion to the cause in such an emergency.

When Clinton found that a large force was close upon him, he took up his position at Monmouth Court House, now Freehold, New Jersey, and prepared to meet the Americans. Washington knew Clinton's movements, and sent word to

Lee at once to attack the British, unless there should be very powerful reasons to the contrary; adding that he himself was bringing up the rest of the army. Lee had joined La Fayette and was now in command of the advance. La Fayette was eager to move upon the enemy.

"You do not know British soldiers," said Lee; "we cannot stand against them. We shall certainly be driven back at first, and we must be cautious."

"Perhaps so," said La Fayette. "But we have beaten British soldiers, and we can do it again."

Soon after, one of Washington's aids appeared for intelligence, and La Fayette, in despair at Lee's inaction, sent the messenger to urge Washington to come at once to the front; that he was needed. Washington was already on the way, before the messenger reached him, when he was met by a little fifer boy, who cried out: —

"They are all coming this way, your honor."

"Who are coming, my little man?" asked General Knox, who was riding by Washington.

"Why, our boys, your honor, our boys, and the British right after them."

"Impossible!" exclaimed Washington, and he galloped to a hill just ahead. To his amazement and dismay, he saw his men retreating. He lost not an instant, but, putting spurs to his horse, dashed forward. After him flew the officers who had been riding by his side, but they could not

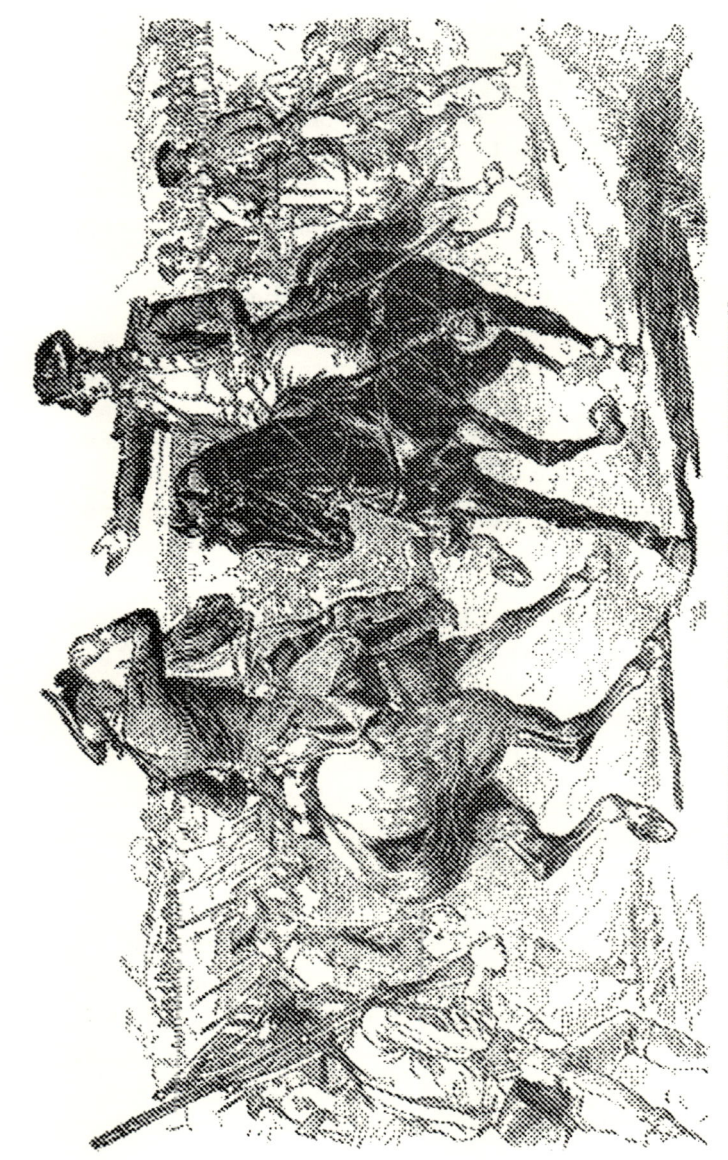

WASHINGTON REBUKING LEE, AT MONMOUTH.

overtake him. His horse, covered with foam, shot down the road over a bridge and up the hill beyond. The retreating column saw him come. The men knew him; they stopped; they made way for the splendid-looking man, as he, their leader, rode headlong into the midst of them. Lee was there, ordering the retreat, and Washington drew his rein as he came upon him. A moment of terrible silence — then Washington burst out, his eyes flashing: —

"What, sir, is the meaning of this?"

"Sir, sir," stammered Lee.

"I desire to know, sir, the meaning of this disorder and confusion?"

Lee, enraged now by Washington's towering passion, made an angry reply. He declared that the whole affair was against his opinion.

"You are a poltroon!" flashed back Washington, with an oath. "Whatever your opinion may have been, I expected my orders to be obeyed."

"These men cannot face the British grenadiers," answered Lee.

"They can do it, and they shall!" exclaimed Washington, galloping off to survey the ground. Presently he came back; his wrath had gone down in the presence of the peril to the army. He would waste no strength in cursing Lee.

"Will you retain the command here, or shall I?" he asked. "If you will, I will return to the main body and have it formed on the next height."

"It is equal to me where I command," said Lee, sullenly.

"Then remain here," said Washington. "I expect you to take proper means for checking the enemy."

"Your orders shall be obeyed, and I shall not be the first to leave the ground," replied Lee, with spirit.

The rest of the day the battle raged, and when night came the enemy had been obliged to fall back, and Washington determined to follow up his success in the morning. He directed all the troops to lie on their arms where they were. He himself lay stretched on the ground beneath a tree, his cloak wrapped about him. About midnight, an officer came near with a message, but hesitated, reluctant to waken him.

"Advance, sir, and deliver your message," Washington called out; "I lie here to think, and not to sleep."

In the morning, Washington prepared to renew the attack, but the British had slipped away under cover of the darkness, not willing to venture another battle.

Pursuit, except by some cavalry, was unavailing. The men were exhausted. The sun beat down fiercely, and the hot sand made walking difficult. Moreover, the British fleet lay off Sandy Hook, and an advance in that direction would lead the army nearer to the enemy's reënforcements.

Accordingly Washington marched his army to Brunswick, and thence to the Hudson River, crossed it, and encamped again near White Plains.

After the battle of Monmouth, Lee wrote an angry letter to Washington and received a cool one in reply. Lee demanded a court-martial, and Washington at once ordered it. Three charges were made, and Lee was convicted of disobedience of orders in not attacking the enemy on the 28th of June, agreeably to repeated instructions; misbehavior before the enemy on the same day, by making an unnecessary and disorderly retreat; and disrespect to the commander-in-chief. He was suspended from the army for a year, and he never returned to it. Long after his death facts were brought to light which make it seem more than probable that General Lee was so eaten up by vanity, by jealousy of Washington, and by a love of his profession above a love of his country, that he was a traitor at heart, and that instead of being ready to sacrifice himself for his country, he was ready to sacrifice the country to his own willful ambition and pride.

But his disgrace was the end of all opposition to Washington. From that time there was no question as to who was at the head of the army and the people.

CHAPTER XX.

THE LAST CAMPAIGN.

THE battle of Monmouth was the last great battle before the final victory at Yorktown. The three and a half years which intervened, however, were busy years for Washington. He was obliged to settle disputes between the French and American officers, to order the disposition of the forces, and to give his attention to all the suggestions of plans for action. He was greatly concerned that Congress should be growing weak and inefficient. Here was a man, whom some had foolishly supposed to be aiming at supreme power, only anxious that the civil government should be strengthened. He saw very clearly that while the separate States were looking after their several affairs, the Congress which represented the whole country was losing its influence and power. "I think our political system," he wrote, "may be compared to the mechanism of a clock, and that we should derive a lesson from it; for it answers no good purpose to keep the smaller wheels in order, if the greater one, which is the support and prime mover of the whole, is neglected."

He was indignant at the manner in which Congressmen, and others who were concerned in the affairs of the country, spent their time in Philadelphia. "An assembly," he said, "a concert, a dinner, a supper, that will cost three or four hundred pounds, will not only take off men from acting in this business, but even from thinking of it; while a great part of the officers of our army, from absolute necessity, are quitting the service; and the more virtuous few, rather than do this, are sinking by sure degrees into beggary and want." How simply he himself lived may be seen by the jocose letter which he wrote to a friend, inviting him to dine with him at headquarters. The letter is addressed to Dr. Cochran, surgeon-general in the army: —

"DEAR DOCTOR, — I have asked Mrs. Cochran and Mrs. Livingston to dine with me to-morrow; but am I not in honor bound to apprise them of their fare? As I hate deception, even where the imagination only is concerned, I will. It is needless to premise that my table is large enough to hold the ladies. Of this they had ocular proof yesterday. To say how it is usually covered is rather more essential; and this shall be the purport of my letter.

"Since our arrival at this happy spot, we have had a ham, sometimes a shoulder of bacon, to grace the head of the table; a piece of roast beef adorns the foot; and a dish of beans or greens, almost imperceptible, decorates the centre. When the cook has a mind to cut a figure, which I presume will be the case to-morrow, we have two beefsteak pies, or dishes of crabs, dividing the space and reducing the distance between dish and dish, to about six feet, which, without them, would be near twelve feet apart. Of late he has had the surprising sagacity to discover that apples will make pies; and it is a question if, in the violence of his efforts, we do not get one of apples, instead of having both of beefsteaks. If the ladies can put up with such entertainment, and will submit to partake of it on plates once tin but now iron (not become so by the labor of scouring), I shall be happy to see them; and am, dear Doctor, yours."

The main activity of the two armies in the last years of the war was in the South, where General Gates, and after him General Greene, were engaged in a contest with Lord Cornwallis. Washington, meanwhile, kept his position on the Hudson, where he could watch the movements of the enemy still in strong force in New York. The care of the whole country was on his shoulders, for, except by his personal endeavors, it was impossible for the armies to secure even what support they did receive from Congress and the state governments. The letters written by Washington during this period disclose the numberless difficulties which he was obliged to meet and overcome. He was the one man to whom all turned, and he gave freely of himself. How completely he ignored his own personal interests may be seen by an incident which occurred at Mount Vernon.

Several British vessels had sailed up the Chesapeake and Potomac, and had pillaged the country roundabout. When these vessels lay off Mount Vernon, the manager of Washington's estate, anxious to save the property under his charge, went out and bought off the marauders by a liberal gift. Washington wrote at once, rebuking him for his conduct. In the letter, he used these words:—

"I am very sorry to hear of your loss: I am a little sorry to hear of my own; but that which gives me most concern is that you should go on board the enemy's vessel and furnish them with refreshments. It would have been a less painful circumstance to me to have heard that, in consequence of your non-compliance with their request, they had burnt my house and laid the plantation in ruins. You ought to have considered yourself as my representative, and should have reflected on the bad example of communicating with the enemy, and making a voluntary offer of refreshments to them with a view to prevent a conflagration. It was not in your power, I acknowledge, to prevent them from sending a flag on shore, and you did right to meet it; but you should, in the same instant that the business of it was unfolded, have declared explicitly that it was improper for you to yield to their request; after which, if they had proceeded to help themselves by force, you could but have submitted; and being unprovided for defense, this was to be preferred to a feeble opposition, which only serves as a pretext to burn and destroy."

In July, 1781, Washington's army, which was

watching Sir Henry Clinton in New York, was reënforced by the French troops, and at the same time a French squadron cruised off the coast ready to coöperate. General Greene was crowding Lord Cornwallis in the South and edging him up into Virginia, and the design was to keep the two British armies apart, and defeat each. But the siege of New York was likely to be a long one, and the French admiral had orders to repair to the West Indies in the fall. So time was precious.

Accordingly, Washington determined to mass his troops in Virginia, unite the northern and southern armies, and, in conjunction with the French fleet, completely crush Cornwallis. It was necessary, however, that Clinton, in New York, should suspect nothing of this scheme, or else he, too, would join Cornwallis. The change of plan was carried out with great skill. Letters were written detailing imaginary movements, and these letters fell into the hands of the British general, who supposed that great preparations were making to attack him in New York. Meanwhile, a few troops only were left in camp at White Plains, while the rest of the army crossed the Hudson and moved rapidly to Virginia. It was not until the two armies were within reach of each other that Clinton learned what had really been going on.

Washington took this opportunity to make a flying visit to Mount Vernon. It was the first time he had been there since he left it to attend that meeting of the Continental Congress at which he had been chosen commander-in-chief. He had never lost sight of his home, however. Thither his thoughts often turned, and many a time, amid the anxieties and cares of his burdensome life, he looked with longing toward the quiet haven of Mount Vernon. He wrote weekly to the manager of his estate, and he gave him one general rule of conduct in this wise: "Let the hospitality of the house, with respect to the poor, be kept up. Let no one go away hungry. If any of this kind of people should be in want of corn, supply their necessities, provided it does not encourage them in idleness."

He stayed but a couple of days at Mount Vernon, where he was joined by Count Rochambeau, and then he hastened to the headquarters of the army at Williamsburg. It was now the middle of September. Cornwallis was at Yorktown, and everything depended on the ability of the combined French and American forces to capture his army before he could be reënforced by Clinton. The leading generals of the American army were there, eagerly directing operations, and Washington was at the front superintending the works, for the men were fighting Cornwallis with the spade as well as with cannon. Washington put the match to the first gun that was fired. One who was in the army at the time relates an incident that came under his notice: —

"A considerable cannonading from the enemy; one shot killed three men, and mortally wounded another. While the Rev. Mr. Evans, our chaplain, was standing near the commander-in-chief, a shot struck the ground so near as to cover his hat with sand. Being much agitated, he took off his hat, and said, 'See here, General!' 'Mr. Evans,' replied his excellency, with his usual composure, 'you 'd better carry that home and show it to your wife and children.'"

Indeed, it seemed to many that Washington bore a charmed life, and it was often said that he was under the special protection of God. He was fearless, and constantly exposed to danger, but his constant escapes made him cool and self-possessed, and the admiration of his men. He was excited by the events which were hurrying the war to the close, and he watched with intense earnestness the several assaults which were made on the works. Once he had dismounted and was standing by Generals Knox and Lincoln at the grand battery. It was not a safe place, for, though they were behind a fortification, it was quite possible for shot to enter the opening through which they were looking. One of his aids, growing nervous, begged him to leave, for the place was very much exposed.

"If you think so," said Washington, "you are at liberty to step back." Presently a ball did strike the cannon, and, rolling off, fell at Washington's feet. General Knox seized him by the arm.

"My dear General," said he, "we can't spare you yet."

"It's a spent ball," replied Washington, coolly. "No harm is done." He watched the action until the redoubts which his men had been assaulting were taken; then he drew a long breath of relief and turned to Knox.

"The work is done," he said emphatically; "and well done."

The siege was short, the work was sharp, for it was full of enthusiasm and hope, and when, on October 19, the army of Lord Cornwallis surrendered to General Washington, there was a tumult of rejoicing in camp which was long remembered. Washington issued orders that the army should give thanks to God. "Divine service," he said, "is to be performed to-morrow in the several brigades and divisions. The commander-in-chief earnestly recommends that the troops not on duty should universally attend, with that seriousness of deportment and gratitude of heart which the recognition of such reiterated and astonishing interpositions of Providence demand of us."

The officers of the combined armies spent some time in the neighborhood, and there was a great ball given at Fredericksburg by the citizens of the place. The most distinguished guest was the mother of Washington, then seventy-four years old, who came into the room leaning on the arm of her son. She was quiet and dignified, as one after another of the French officers made his bow and his complimentary speech; but I think there must have been a great deal of motherly pride in her heart, though it is said that when her George came to see her alone after the victory at Yorktown, she spoke to him of his health, marked the lines of care on his face, spoke of his early days, and gave him a mother's caution, but said nothing of the glory he had won. To the last he was her boy, and not America's hero.

CHAPTER XXI.

WASHINGTON RESIGNS HIS COMMISSION.

AFTER the surrender of Yorktown and the departure of the French, Washington established his headquarters at Newburgh on the Hudson. There he remained with the army until it was disbanded; and the house in which he lived is carefully preserved and shown as an historical museum.

There is a pleasant story of La Fayette's affectionate remembrance of the life there. Just before his death, which occurred in 1834, he gave a dinner party in Paris to the American Minister and some friends who had been old associates. Later in the evening, when the hour for supper came, the guests were ushered into a room which was in strange contrast with the elegance of the apartments they had been in. The ceiling was low, with large beams crossing it; there was a single small, uncurtained window, and several small doors. It looked more like an old-fashioned Dutch kitchen than a room in a French house. A long, rough table was meagrely set. A dish of meat stood on it, some uncouth-looking pastry, and wine in decanters and bottles, ready to be poured out into glasses and camp-mugs.

"Do you know where we are now?" asked La Fayette as his companions looked about puzzled, and as if in a dream. "Ah! the seven doors and one window! and the silver camp-goblets! We are at Washington's headquarters on the Hudson, fifty years ago!" He had reproduced the room as a surprise to his friends.

Peace did not come at once after Yorktown; there was still fighting in a desultory way, but all knew that the end was not far off. Yet the soldiers could not go back to their homes, and Congress was shamefully remiss about paying them. Murmurs deep and loud arose, and Washington suffered keenly from the neglect shown to the army. It required all his patience and tact to keep the murmurs from breaking out into violent action. With no military duty to perform, and with the impatience of men who were suffering injustice, the officers and men began to form all sorts of plans.

One of the officers — and how many agreed with him is not known, but the sentiment easily took this form — one of the officers wrote to Washington that it was clear that Congress was a failure. The army had won independence, but no reliance could be placed on the government. How much more stable was the government of England! Would not such a government be after all the best for America? It might not be necessary to call the head of the government a king, though even that title many would prefer, but the head ought to have the power of a king. There was much more to the same effect, and the letter was really a feeler to see how Washington would look upon such a movement, which, of course, aimed to make him the monarch of the new nation. Washington did not hesitate a moment, but wrote a letter which must have made the officer's ears tingle, however honest he may have been in his opinion. Washington said: —

"With a mixture of great surprise and astonishment, I have read with attention the sentiments you have submitted to my perusal. Be assured, sir, no occurrence in the course of the war has given me more painful sensations than your information of there being such ideas existing in the army as you have expressed and I must view with abhorrence and reprehend with severity. For the present, the communication of them will rest in my own bosom, unless some further agitation of the matter shall make a disclosure necessary. I am much at a loss to conceive what part of my conduct could have given encouragement to an address, which, to me, seems big with the greatest mischief that can befall any country. If I am not deceived in the knowledge of myself, you could not have found a person to whom your schemes are more disagreeable. At the same time, in justice to my own feelings, I must add that no man possesses a more sincere wish to see ample justice done to the army than I do; and as far as my powers and influence in a constitutional way extend, they shall be employed to the utmost of my abilities to effect it, should there be any occasion. Let me conjure you, then, if you have any regard for your country, concern for yourself or posterity, or respect for me, to banish these thoughts from your mind, and never communicate, as from yourself or any one else, a sentiment of the like nature."

A graver peril arose, and Washington redeemed his promise to stand by the army. In spite of the united effort of the army and its friends in Congress, no satisfactory arrangement was made for paying the long-delayed wages due to the soldiers. On March 10, 1783, a notice was issued in the camp at Newburgh, calling a meeting of the officers. The notice was not signed by any name, and with it was sent out an address which rehearsed the wrongs suffered by the army, and hinted that the time had come when the soldiers must take matters into their own hands and compel Congress to attend to their demands. It was an appeal to which the officers were ready to listen, and every one was in so excited a condition that it was impossible to say what might not be done.

Washington, at any rate, saw there was great danger, and he at once seized the occasion. He issued an order calling attention to the address, and asking that the meeting should be postponed four days and then should convene at his invitation. This was to give the men time to cool off. When the day came, Washington, as soon as the meeting was called to order, made a long and powerful speech. He was not a ready speaker, and so, feeling the importance of the occasion, he had written out what he had to say, and he began to read it to the officers. He had read only a sentence, when he stopped, took out his spectacles, and said, as he put them on: —

"Gentlemen, you will pardon me for putting on my glasses. I have grown gray in your service, and I now find myself growing blind."

It was a simple thing to say, and simply said, but it touched the soldiers, and made them very tender to their commander, and more ready even than before to listen to his counsel. Washington went on to say: —

"If my conduct heretofore has not evinced to you that I have been a faithful friend to the army, my declaration of it at this time would be equally unavailing and improper. But, as I was among the first who embarked in the cause of our common country; as I have never left your side one moment, save when called from you on public duty; as I have been the constant companion and witness of your distresses, and not among the last to feel and acknowledge your merits; as I have considered my own military reputation as inseparably connected with that of the army; as my heart has ever expanded with joy, when I have heard its praises, and my indignation has arisen, when the mouth of detraction has been opened against it; it can scarcely be supposed, at this late stage of the war, that I am indifferent to its interests."

He used all his personal influence to heal the breach between the army and Congress, and he brought the officers back to a more reasonable mind. All the while he was writing to members of Congress and doing his utmost to bring about a just treatment of the army.

When the time came to disband the army, Washington, ready as he was to go back to his home, could not forget that the work of the past seven years would not be completed until the people which had become independent was united under a strong government. He was the foremost man in the country; he was also profoundly aware of the difficulties through which the people were yet to pass, and he addressed a long letter to the governors of the several states. Congress was weak and unable to take the lead. The states were each provided with governments, and were the real powers, but Washington saw clearly that it would not do to have thirteen independent governments in the country, each looking only after its own interests. So in this letter he tried to show the states the importance of four things:

1. An indissoluble union of the states under one head.

2. The payment of all the debts contracted by the country in the war.

3. The establishment of a uniform militia system throughout the country. He did not advise having a standing army, but he thought all the

men should be drilled in their neighborhoods, formed into companies, and be ready in any peril to take up arms again.

4. The cultivation of a spirit of confidence between different parts of the country. He had seen so much jealousy and prejudice that he knew how dangerous these were to the peace of the country.

At last the time came when the army was disbanded. A few of the troops only and their officers went with Washington to New York when the British left the city. There was rejoicing everywhere; but it was a sorrowful moment when Washington took leave in person of the officers who had stood by him through the long, dreary years of the war. He was about to leave the city to be ferried across the North River to the Jersey shore, and his old friends gathered to say goodby at Fraunce's Tavern, in Broad Street. When he entered the room he could scarcely command his voice. He said a word or two, and they all drank a farewell toast, as the custom was in those days. Then Washington said: "I cannot come to each of you to take my leave, but shall be obliged if each of you will come and take me by the hand."

General Knox stood nearest, and he held out his hand. The tears were in Washington's eyes as he turned to his old comrade and grasped his hand. He drew the strong man to him — Knox was nearly twenty years younger than Washington, and very dear to him — and kissed him. Not a word could either of them speak. Another general followed and another, each greeted with the same affection; and then Washington left the room, passed through the corps of infantry which stood on guard, and walked to Whitehall, followed by the whole company, a silent procession. He entered the barge, turned as the boat pushed off, and waved his hat in silent adieu. The officers returned the salute in the same way, and then turned and in silence marched back to Fraunce's.

Washington went to Philadelphia. Congress was in session at Annapolis, but the Treasury was in Philadelphia. On receiving his commission as commander-in-chief, Washington had announced that he would receive no money for services, but would keep an exact account of all his expenses. That account he had kept as carefully and scrupulously as any book-keeper in a bank, and he now rendered it to the comptroller of the treasury. It was in his own handwriting, every item set down and explained. I know of few incidents in Washington's career which show the character of the man better than this. He held that a sacred trust had been reposed in him, and he meant to be faithful in the least particular.

On December 23, 1783, Congress was assembled at Annapolis. The gallery was filled with ladies. The governor, council, and legislature of Maryland, several officers, and the consul-general of France were on the floor. The members of Congress were seated and wore their hats to signify that they represented the government. The spectators stood with bare heads. General Washington entered and was conducted by the secretary of Congress to a seat. When all was quiet, General Mifflin, who was then president of Congress, turned to Washington and said: "The United States, in Congress assembled, is prepared to receive the communications of the commander-in-chief."

Washington rose and read a short address, in which he resigned his commission. He delivered the paper into the hands of the president, who replied with a little speech; and Washington was now a private citizen. The next day he left Annapolis, and made all haste to return to his beloved Mount Vernon.

CHAPTER XXII.

MR. WASHINGTON.

IT was hard for Washington at first to forget that he was no longer commander-in-chief. He had so long been accustomed to wake early, and at once begin to think of the cares of the day, that it was a novel sensation to discover that he had no cares beyond looking after his estate. It chanced that the winter of 1783–84 was a very severe one. The roads were blocked with snow, the streams were frozen, and Washington found himself almost a prisoner at Mount Vernon. He was not even able to go to Fredericksburg to see his mother, until the middle of February. He was not sorry for his enforced quiet. It left him leisure to look over his papers and enjoy the company of his wife and his wife's grandchildren, whom he had adopted as his own children. His public papers had been put into the hands of Colonel Richard Varick, in 1781, and they were now returned to him, arranged and classified and copied into volumes, in a manner to delight the methodical soul of their author.

As the spring came on, and the snow and ice melted, the roads were again open, and Mount

Vernon was soon busy with its old hospitality. Washington foresaw that he would have plenty of visitors, but he did not mean to let his life be at the mercy of everybody, and he meant to keep up his regular habits and his plain living. "My manner of living is plain," he wrote to a friend, "and I do not mean to be put out of it. A glass of wine and a bit of mutton are always ready, and such as will be content to partake of them are always welcome. Those who expect more will be disappointed."

The house at Mount Vernon before this time had been very much like that in which Washington was born; now he found it necessary to enlarge it, and accordingly added an extension at each end, making it substantially as it now appears. He was his own architect, and he drew every plan and specification for the workmen with his own hand. He amused himself also with laying out the grounds about his house, and planting trees, — a great pleasure to him. Every morning he arose early, and dispatched his correspondence before breakfast, which was at half-past seven. His horse stood ready at the door, and as soon as breakfast was over, he was in the saddle, visiting the various parts of his estate. Sometimes he went hunting, for he never lost his fondness for the chase. He dined at three o'clock, and usually spent the afternoon in the library, sometimes working at his papers till nine o'clock;

but when not pressed by business, and when his house was full of guests, he spent the evening with them. If he was alone with his family, he read aloud to them; and very often on Sundays, when they could not go to church, he read aloud a sermon and prayers.

Guests crowded upon him, and he was especially glad to see his old comrades. A visit from La Fayette was the occasion of a very gay time, when Mount Vernon was full of visitors, and the days were given to sport.

Washington had constant applications from persons who wished to write his life or paint his portrait. There was a sculptor named Wright who undertook to get a model of Washington's face. "Wright came to Mount Vernon," so Washington tells the story, "with the singular request that I should permit him to take a model of my face, in plaster of Paris, to which I consented with some reluctance. He oiled my features, and placing me flat upon my back, upon a cot, proceeded to daub my face with the plaster. Whilst I was in this ludicrous attitude, Mrs. Washington entered the room, and seeing my face thus overspread with plaster, involuntarily exclaimed. Her cry excited in me a disposition to smile, which gave my mouth a slight twist, or compression of the lips, that is now observable in the busts which Wright afterward made." A more successful sculptor was Houdon, who was commissioned by

Virginia to make a statue of Washington. He also took a plaster model, and the fine statue which he made stands in Richmond. A portrait painter, named Pine, also paid a visit to Mount Vernon about this time with a letter from one of Washington's friends to whom Washington wrote during Pine's visit: —

" 'In for a penny, in for a pound,' is an old adage. I am so hackneyed to the touches of the painter's pencil that I am now altogether at their beck, and sit, like 'patience on a monument,' whilst they are delineating the lines of my face. It is a proof among many others of what habit and custom can effect. At first I was as impatient at the request, and as restive under the operation, as a colt is of the saddle. The next time I submitted very reluctantly, but with less flouncing. Now no dray moves more readily to the thill than I do to the painter's chair. It may easily be conceived, therefore, that I yielded a ready obedience to your request, and to the views of Mr. Pine."

Washington was a most considerate and courteous host. He was very fond of young people, but his silent ways and the reputation which he enjoyed as a great man made it difficult for the young always to be easy in his presence. The story is told of his coming into a room once, when dancing was going on, and the sport suddenly ceased. Washington begged the young people to go on, but they refused until he left the room. Then, after they felt free again to dance, he came back and peeped through the open door.

He was very apt to affect older people in the same way. He was a large man, with large hands and feet, and eyes that looked steadily at one. When not speaking he was very apt to forget there were other people in the room, and his lips would move as he talked to himself while thinking hard upon some matter. But he did not neglect people. One of his visitors tells this story: "The first evening I spent under the wing of his hospitality, we sat a full hour at table, by ourselves, without the least interruption, after the family had retired. I was extremely oppressed with a severe cold and excessive coughing, contracted from the exposure of a harsh winter journey. He pressed me to use some remedies, but I declined doing so. As usual, after retiring, my coughing increased. When some time had elapsed, the door of my room was gently opened, and, on drawing my bed-curtains, to my utter astonishment I beheld Washington himself standing at my bedside, with a bowl of hot tea in his hand. I was mortified and distressed beyond expression."

Although Washington had now retired to Mount Vernon, and seemed perfectly willing to spend the rest of his days as a country gentleman, it was impossible for him to do so. The leaders of the country needed him, and he was himself too deeply interested in affairs to shut his eyes and ears. He was especially interested in the western country, which then meant the Ohio Valley and the region bordered by the Great Lakes. In the autumn of 1784, he made a tour beyond the Alleghanies, for the purpose of looking after the lands which he owned there; but he looked about him not only as a land-owner, but as a wise, far-seeing statesman.

It was a wild journey to take in those days. Washington traveled nearly seven hundred miles on horseback, and had to carry camping conveniences and many of his supplies on pack-horses. He had especially in mind to see if there might be a way of connecting by a canal the water system of Virginia with the Western rivers. After he came back, he wrote a long letter to the governor of Virginia, in which he gave the result of his observation and reflection. He was not merely considering how a profitable enterprise could be undertaken, but he was thinking how necessary it was to bind the western country to the eastern in order to strengthen the Union. Many people had crossed the mountains and were scattered in the Mississippi Valley. They found the Mississippi River a stream easy to sail down, but the Spaniards held the mouth of the river, and if the latter chose to make friends with those western settlers, they might easily estrange them from the eastern states. Besides this, Great Britain was reaching down toward this last territory from Canada. In every way, it seemed to him of importance that good roads and good water communication should bind the East and the West together. He thought Virginia was the state to do this. It extended then far to the westward, and it had great rivers flowing to the sea. It was the most important state in the country, and it was very natural that Washington should look to it to carry out his grand ideas; for the separate states had the power at that time — Congress was unable to do anything. It is interesting to see how Washington, who thought he could go back to Mount Vernon and be a planter, was unable to keep his mind from working upon a great plan which intended the advantage of a vast number of people. He was made to care for great things, and he cared for them naturally.

CHAPTER XXIII.

CALLED TO THE HELM.

WHILE Washington was busy planting trees at Mount Vernon and making excursions to see his western lands, the country was like a vessel which had no captain or pilot, drifting into danger. During the War for Independence, one of the greatest difficulties which Washington had to overcome was the unwillingness of the several states to act together as one nation. They called themselves the United States of America, but they were very loosely united. Congress was the only body that held them together, and Congress had no power to make the states do what they did not care to do. So long as they all were fighting for independence, they managed to hold together; but as soon as the war was over and the states were recognized as independent, it was very hard to get them to do anything as one nation. Every state was looking out for itself, and afraid that the others might gain some advantage over it.

This could not go on forever. They must be either wholly independent of one another or more closely united. The difficulty was more apparent where two states were neighbors. Virginia and

Massachusetts might manage to live apart, though in that case troubles would be sure to arise, but how could Virginia and Maryland maintain their individual independence? The Chesapeake and Potomac seemed to belong to one as much as to the other; and when foreign vessels came up the stream, was each state to have its own rules and regulations? No. They must treat strangers at any rate in some way that would not make each the enemy of the other.

These two states felt this so strongly that they appointed a commission to consider what could be done. Washington was a member of the commission, and asked all the gentlemen to his house. They not only discussed the special subject committed to them, but they looked at the whole matter of the regulation of commerce in a broad way, and agreed to propose to the two states to appoint other commissioners, who should advise with Congress and ask all the states of the Union to send delegates to a meeting where they could arrange some system by which all the states should act alike in their treatment of foreign nations and of each other.

That was exactly what Congress ought to have been able to do, but could not, because nobody paid any attention to it. Nor did this meeting, which was called at Annapolis in September, 1786, accomplish very much. Only five states sent delegates, and these delegates were so carefully instructed not to do much, that it was impossible for the convention to settle affairs. Still, it was a step forward. It was very clear to the delegates that a general convention of all the states was necessary, and so they advised another meeting at which all the thirteen states should be represented, and the whole subject of the better union of the States should be considered.

This meeting, which was the great Constitutional Convention of 1787, was held in Philadelphia, and to it Virginia sent George Washington as one of her delegates. He was heart and soul in favor of the movement. It was what he had been urging on all his correspondents for a long time. He was at first reluctant to go back into public life after having so completely retired; but as soon as he saw that it was his duty to accept the appointment, he set to work to qualify himself for taking part in the deliberations of the convention. Probably no one in America understood better than he the character of Americans and the special dangers through which the country was passing; but several, no doubt, were better informed about the practical working of government and about the history of other confederations. He had never been very much of a reader of books, but he had been a member for many years of the Virginia House of Burgesses, and so knew how government was carried on on a small scale, and now he began to read diligently and to compare accounts of ancient and modern political unions. He made abstracts of them, and, in fact, went to work as if he were at school, so in earnest was he to learn this important lesson.

On May 9, 1787, Washington set out from Mount Vernon in his carriage for Philadelphia. He was a famous man and could not go to the convention without attracting attention. So, when he reached Chester, in Pennsylvania, he was met by General Mifflin, who was then Speaker of the Assembly of Pennsylvania, and by various public men, who escorted him on the way. At the ferry across the Schuylkill, where Gray's Ferry Bridge now is, he was met by a company of light horse, and so entered the city. One of his first errands was to call on Benjamin Franklin, who was President of Pennsylvania, as the governor was then called. No doubt they talked long and earnestly about the work before them, for they were the two most eminent men in the convention.

Washington was made the presiding officer of the convention. For four months it met from day to day, engaged in the great work of forming the Constitution under which we are now governed. There were many long and earnest debates; and the members felt the importance of the work upon which they were engaged. At last, the Constitution was formed. It was not satisfactory to everybody, but the members all agreed to sign it, and recommend it to the country for adoption.

George Washington, as president of the convention, was the first to set his name down; and there is a tradition that as he took the pen in his hand he arose from his seat, considered a moment, and then said: —

"Should the states reject this excellent Constitution, the probability is that an opportunity will never again be offered to cancel another in peace; the next will be drawn in blood."

Washington, as president of the convention, was directed to draw up a letter, stating what the convention had done, and send it with the Constitution to Congress. This he did. He was not entirely satisfied with the Constitution, as he wrote to Patrick Henry: "I wish the Constitution which is offered had been more perfect; but I sincerely believe it is the best that could be obtained at this time. And, as a constitutional door is opened for amendments hereafter, the adoption of it, under the present circumstances of the Union, is, in my opinion, desirable."

He said at first that he should not say anything for or against the Constitution. If it were good, it would work its way; if bad, it would recoil on those who drew it up. Perhaps he thought it was not becoming in those who discussed its parts and finally signed it, to do anything more than send it out and leave the people to do what they would with it. But he could not keep silent long. Everybody was debating it; the principal members of the convention were defending it; there was danger that it would not be adopted, and soon Washington, in his letters, was using arguments in support of it. There is no doubt that his name at the head of the paper did a great deal toward inducing people to accept it. It was more than a year before enough states had adopted the Constitution to make it the law of the land, but as time went on, and it was more certain that the new government would go into operation, the question arose as to who should be the first President of the United States. It can hardly be called a question; at any rate, it was answered at once by all. Every one named Washington, and his friends began to write to him as if there could be no doubt on this point. The most distinguished advocate of the new Constitution, Alexander Hamilton, who had been one of Washington's aids in the war, wrote to him: —

"I take it for granted, sir, you have concluded to comply with what will, no doubt, be the general call of your country in relation to the new government. You will permit me to say that it is indispensable you should lend yourself to its first operations. It is to little purpose to have introduced a system, if the weightiest influence is not given to its firm establishment in the outset."

Washington was by no means elated at the prospect. On the contrary, he was extremely reluctant to be president. He was not old; he was fifty-seven years of age when the election took place, but his hard life as a soldier had broken his constitution, and the cares and anxieties he had undergone had made him feel old. "At my time of life," he wrote to La Fayette, "and under my circumstances, the increasing infirmities of nature and the growing love of retirement do not permit me to entertain a wish beyond that of living and dying an honest man on my own farm. Let those follow the pursuits of ambition and fame who have a keener relish for them, or who may have more years in store for the enjoyment." He was perfectly sincere in saying this. He knew that some people would not believe him, and would assert that he was only saying all this to get the credit of humility; but his best friends believed him, and to one of these he wrote: "If I should receive the appointment, and if I should be prevailed upon to accept it, the acceptance would be attended with more diffidence and reluctance than ever I experienced before in my life. It would be, however, with a fixed and sole determination of lending whatever assistance might be in my power to promote the public weal, in hopes that, at a convenient and early period, my services might be dispensed with, and that I might be permitted once more to retire, to pass an unclouded evening, after the stormy day of life, in the bosom of domestic tranquillity."

There never was any doubt about the people's choice. Every vote was cast for Washington.

CHAPTER XXIV.

PRESIDENT WASHINGTON.

It was on April 16, 1789, that Washington left Mount Vernon for New York, where Congress first met, and where he was to be inaugurated president. The country all along the route was eager to see him, and at every place through which he passed there were processions and triumphal arches and ringing of bells. Some of the signs of welcome were queer, and some were beautiful and touching. When he crossed the Schuylkill, there was a series of arches under which he was to ride; and when he came to the first one, a laurel wreath was let down upon his head. The people who arranged that exhibition must have been very anxious as to how it would turn out. At Trenton, where everybody remembered the famous battle he had fought, the women had put up a great triumphal arch resting upon thirteen columns, with a great dome crowned by a sunflower; then, as he rode through, he came upon a company of women and girls who marched toward him, strewing flowers and singing. When he reached New York, guns were fired; and a vast crowd of people, headed by the governor, was waiting to receive him.

Congress had begun its sessions at Federal Hall, which stood where the present Treasury building stands in Wall Street. The day set for the inauguration was April 30. Precisely at noon, the procession moved from the house where Washington was lodged, through what is now Pearl Street and Broad Street, to the Hall. Washington entered the Senate chamber, where John Adams, who was vice-president and therefore presiding over the Senate, received him in the presence of the Senate and House, and then escorted him to a balcony at the front of the hall. A crimson-covered table stood on it, holding a large Bible. Below, Broad Street and Wall Street were packed with people, as were also the windows and the roofs of the houses near by. They set up a great shout as Washington appeared. He came to the front, laid his hand on his heart, and bowed to the people.

The multitude could see the commanding figure of the great general as he stood bareheaded on the balcony. He was dressed in a suit of brown cloth of American manufacture, with knee-breeches and white silk stockings and silver shoe-buckles. His hair was dressed and powdered, as was the custom then. They saw near him John Adams and Robert R. Livingston, the chancellor of the State of New York, and distinguished men — generals and others; but their eyes were bent on Washington. They saw Chancellor Livingston stand as if speaking to him, and the secretary of the Senate holding the open Bible, on which Washington's hand lay. Those nearest could hear the chancellor pronounce the oath of office and Washington's reply, "I swear — so help me, God!" and could see him bow and kiss the Bible.

Then the chancellor stepped forward, waved his hand, and said aloud: "Long live George Washington, President of the United States." At the same time, a flag, as a signal, was run up on the cupola of the Hall. Instantly cannon were fired, bells rung, and the people shouted. Washington saluted them, and then turned back into the Senate chamber, where he read his inaugural address, in a low voice, for he was evidently deeply affected, — great occasions always solemnized him, — and after the address, he went on foot, with many others, to St. Paul's Church, where prayers were read by Dr. Provoost, Bishop of the Episcopal Church, and one of the chaplains of Congress. At night, there were fireworks and bonfires.

Thus, with the good-will of the people and the confidence of all the sections, — however suspicious they might be of one another, — Washington began his career as president. For eight years he remained in office. His character was now so fixed that there is little new to be learned about it from that time forward; but there were many events that made more clear how wise, how just, how honorable, and how faithful to his trust he was. He had been very loath to take upon himself the duties of president, but when once he had been placed in the chair, he let nothing stand in the way of the most thorough discharge of his duties.

Now came into play all those habits which he had been forming from boyhood. As president of the whole people, it was his business to have an oversight of all the interests of the young nation, and, as the first president, he had the opportunity of setting an example to those who were to come after him. It is one of the most excellent gifts to the American people that they should have had for their first president a man so well rounded and so magnanimous as George Washington. There were as yet no political parties, though there were the seeds of parties in the opposite ways in which public men regarded the new Constitution. Washington called to his cabinet men who disliked one another, and who were really as much opposed to one another as if they belonged to antagonistic parties; but they never could draw Washington away from a strict impartiality. He made Thomas Jefferson secretary of state, because he was most thoroughly acquainted with foreign affairs; and he made Alexander Hamilton secretary of the treasury, because he had shown himself the most competent man to plan a way out of the greatest peril which beset the young nation. But Jefferson and Hamilton cordially disliked each other, and were decidedly of opposite ways of thinking.

Washington, however, did not rest contented with choosing the best men to carry on the government. In those days, when the country had only a small population, a small area, and a small business, it was possible for one man to know very much more fully the details of government than it is now. His lifelong habits of methodical industry enabled Washington to get through an amount of work which seems extraordinary. For example, he read from beginning to end all the letters which had passed between Congress and foreign governments since the treaty of peace in 1783, making abstracts and briefs of them, so as to know thoroughly the whole history of the relations of the country to foreign governments. He required from every head of department whom he found in office a report of the state of public business. He treated these reports as he had the foreign correspondence, and in this way he mastered all the internal affairs of the nation. The result was that he had his own judgment about any matter of importance which came up, and was not obliged to follow the lead of the cabinet officers.

There were, of course, only a few public offices to be filled then, and it was quite possible for Washington to know personally most of the men who should be appointed to fill them. He thought this one of the most important parts of his work as president; because he knew well that it is not rules and regulations, but men, that carry on any government or any business, and that, if he could put honest and capable men, who were unselfishly devoted to the country, into all the offices, he would secure a wise administration of the laws. From the first, he began to be besieged by applicants for office, and he made immediately the very sensible rule that he would not give any pledge or encouragement to any applicant. He heard what they and their friends had to say, and then made up his mind deliberately. He had, however, certain principles in his mind which governed him in making appointments, and they were so high and honorable, and show so well the character of the man, that I copy here what he had said with regard to the matter: —

"Scarcely a day passes in which applications of one kind or another do not arrive; insomuch that, had I not early adopted some general principles, I should before this time have been wholly occupied in this business. As it is, I have found the number of answers, which I have been necessitated to give in my own hand, an almost insupportable burden to me. The points in which all these answers have agreed in substance are, that, should it be my lot to go again into public office, I would go without being under any possible engagements of any nature whatsoever; that, so far as I knew my own heart, I would not be in the remotest degree influenced in making nominations by motives arising from the ties of family or blood; and that, on the other hand, three things, in my opinion, ought principally to be regarded, namely: the fitness of characters to fill offices, the comparative claims from the former merits and sufferings in service of the different candidates, and the distribution of appointments in as equal a proportion as might be to persons belonging to the different States in the Union. Without precautions of this kind, I clearly foresaw the endless jealousies and possibly the fatal consequences to which a government, depending altogether on the good-will of the people for its establishment, would certainly be exposed in its early stages. Besides, I thought, whatever the effect might be in pleasing or displeasing any individuals at the present moment, a due concern for my own reputation, not less decisively than a sacred regard to the interests of the community, required that I should hold myself absolutely at liberty to act, while in office, with a sole reference to justice and the public good."

To protect himself from being at everybody's call, and so unable to be of the greatest service, he established certain rules. Every Tuesday, between the hours of three and four, he received whoever might come. Every Friday afternoon Mrs. Washington received with him. At all other times, he could be seen only by special appointment. He never accepted invitations to dinner, and that has been the rule of presidents ever since; but he invited constantly to his own table foreign ministers, members of the government, and other guests. He received no visits on Sunday. He went to church with his family in the morning, and spent the afternoon by himself. The evening he spent with his family and sometimes had with him an intimate friend.

He still kept up his old habit of rising at four and going to bed at nine. Mrs. Washington had a grave little formula with which she used to dismiss visitors in the evening: —

"The General always retires at nine o'clock, and I usually precede him."

His recreation he took chiefly in driving and riding. He never lost his liking for a good horse, and he knew what a good horse was. He had a servant who had been General Braddock's servant, and had been with Washington ever since the battle of the Monongahela. Bishop, as he was named, was a terrible disciplinarian, and devoted to his master's interests. At sunrise every day he would go to the stables, where the boys had been at work since dawn grooming the general's horses. Woe to them if they had been careless! Bishop marched in with a muslin handkerchief in his hand and passed it over the coats of the horses; if a single stain appeared on the muslin, the boy who groomed the horse had to take a thrashing. It was no light matter to groom a horse in those days, for, just as the heads of gentlemen were plastered and bewigged, so the horses were made to undergo what would seem to us now a rather absurd practice. The night before a horse was to be ridden, he was covered from head to foot with a paste made of whiting and other ingredients; then he was well wrapped in cloth and laid to sleep on clean straw. By the next morning the paste had hardened, and it was then vigorously rubbed in, and the horse curried and brushed. The result was a glossy and satiny coat. The hoofs were blackened and polished, the mouth washed, the teeth picked and cleaned, and the horse was then ready to be saddled and brought out.

Mrs. Washington was a domestic, home-loving body, but a lady of great dignity and sweetness of disposition, who moved serenely by the side of her husband, receiving his guests in the same spirit. She never talked about politics, but was evenly courteous to every one. She was like her husband, too, in her exactness and her attention to little details of economy. While she was in the midst of her duties as president's wife, she wrote to one of her family: "I live a very dull life here, and know nothing that passes in the town. I never go to any public place; indeed, I think I am more like a state prisoner than anything else. There are certain bounds set for me which I must not depart from; and, as I cannot do as I like, I am obstinate and stay at home a great deal." But her real heart was at Mount Vernon and in her household affairs. "I send to dear Maria," she writes, "A piece of *chene* to make her a frock, and a piece of muslin, which I hope is long enough for an apron for you. In exchange for it, I beg you will give me a worked muslin apron you have, like my gown that I made just before I left home, of worked muslin, as I wish to make a petticoat to my gown, of the two aprons."

Washington himself never lost sight of Mount Vernon. Just as in his absence, during the war, he required weekly reports from the manager of his plantation, so now he kept up the same practice. Occasionally, when Congress was not in session, he could go home, but his visits were short and rare. It may seem strange to some that a soldier and a statesman like Washington should be also an ardent farmer; but that he was. I suppose the one occupation that Washington loved was farming; in his earlier life there is no doubt that he cared most for a soldier's fortune, but after he was fairly in possession of Mount Vernon, the care of that place became his passion, and for the rest of his life he was first and last a farmer. For my part, I like to think of Washington in this way, for the one indispensable art is the art of agriculture; all other arts are built upon it, and the man who has a piece of land, and can raise from it enough to feed and clothe and shelter himself and his family, is the most independent of men, and has a real place on the earth which he can call his own.

During his presidency, Washington made two tours through the country, — one into the Eastern and one into the Southern States. He was received with special honor in New England, for he was less familiarly known to the people there, and they made a great holiday in every town through which the president passed. By these tours, he made himself acquainted with the needs of the country and with the persons who were the leaders of the people.

But there were parts which he could not visit, yet in which he felt the deepest interest and concern. We have seen how, from time to time, he visited the country beyond the Alleghanies, and how much importance he attached to the settlement of the West. The greatest difficulty in the early days was through the relations which the people had with the Indians. Washington knew the Indians well; he knew how to get along with them, and he knew also what dangerous enemies they were. At the end of his first term as president, it became necessary to send a military expedition to the frontiers, and General St. Clair was placed at the head of it. When he came to bid Washington good-by, his old chief gave him a solemn warning: "You have your instructions from the secretary of war. I had a strict eye to them, and will add but one word: Beware of a surprise! You know how the Indians fight. I repeat it — beware of a surprise!"

But St. Clair was surprised and terribly defeated. It was a bitter disappointment to Washington, who received the news of the disaster one December day when he was at dinner. His private secretary, Mr. Lear, was called out of the room by a servant, who said there was a messenger without who insisted on seeing the president. Mr. Lear went to him and found that he was an officer from St. Clair's army with despatches which he refused to give to any one but President Washington. Mr. Lear went back to the dining-room and whispered this to Washington, who excused himself to the company and went out to hear the officer's news. He came back shortly after and resumed his place at the table, but without explaining the reason of his absence. He was, however, absorbed, as he often was, and muttered to himself; and one of his neighbors caught the words, "I knew it would be so!"

It was an evening when Mrs. Washington was holding a reception, and the gentlemen, when leaving the dining-room, went directly into the drawing-room. Washington went with them. He was calm and showed no signs of disturbance. He spoke as usual to every one, and at last the guests had gone. Mrs. Washington also retired, and the General was left alone with his secretary. He was silent at first, walking to and fro in the room. Then he took a seat by the fire, and motioned Mr. Lear to sit by him. He could no longer contain himself; he must have some relief, and suddenly he burst out: "It's all over! St. Clair's defeated! routed! The officers nearly all killed; the men by wholesale; the rout complete — too shocking to think of, and a surprise into the bargain!" He jerked out the sentences as if he were in pain. He got up and walked up and down again like a caged lion, stood still, and once more burst out in passionate speech: "Yes, *here*, on this very spot I took leave of him; I wished him success and honor. 'You have your instructions from the secretary of war,' said I. 'I had a strict eye to them, and will add but one word: BEWARE OF A SURPRISE! You know how the Indians fight; I repeat it — BEWARE OF A SURPRISE!' He went off with that, my last warning, thrown into his ears. And yet! — To suffer that army to be cut to pieces, butchered, tomahawked, by a surprise — the very thing I guarded him against!" — and the strong man threw up his hands while he shook with terrible emotion: "He's worse than a murderer! How can he answer for it to his country! The blood of the slain is upon him — the curse of widows and orphans — the curse of Heaven!"

Mr. Lear was dumb. He had never seen or heard Washington like this. It was a pent-up volcano bursting forth. Washington himself recovered his control. He sat down again. He was silent. He felt, as a strong man does who has for a moment broken the bounds of restraint, a noble shame, not at his indignation, but at having for a moment thus given way. "This must not go beyond this room," he said presently, in a quiet, almost whispered tone. Then he added, after a pause: "General St. Clair shall have justice. I looked hastily through the despatches; saw the whole disaster, but not all the particulars. I will receive him without displeasure; I will hear him without prejudice; he shall have full justice."

Washington kept his word. Perhaps all the more for this outbreak, he determined that St. Clair should be treated with scrupulous justice. But the incident illustrates the character of Washington. Deep down in his nature was a passionate regard for law, for obedience, for strict accountability. It was this which made him in minor matters so punctual, so orderly, so precise in his accounts; in larger matters, it made him unselfishly and wholly consecrated to the country which trusted him, just in all his dealings, and the soul of honor. This consuming passion for law made him govern himself, keep in restraint the fierce wrath which leaped up within him, and measure his acts and words with an iron will. The two notable scenes when his anger blazed out and burned up his self-control as if it were a casing of straw were caused by Lee's faithlessness at Monmouth and St. Clair's carelessness. On each of these occasions, it was not an offense against himself which woke his terrible wrath; it was an offense against the country, against God; for in the moment of his anger he saw each of these two men false to the trust reposed in him.

Yet the difficulties with the Indians were as nothing to the perils which beset the country in its intercourse with Europe. At that time, the United States was almost a part of Europe. All its business was with France and England. It had declared and achieved political independence, but was nevertheless connected by a thousand ties of commerce, law, and custom with the Old World. The fierce revolution in France was in part set in flame by the example of America; and when war broke out between England and France, there was scarcely a man in America who did not take sides in his mind with one country or the other. There was the greatest possible danger that the country would be drawn into the quarrels of Europe.

In the midst of all these commotions, when the very members of his cabinet were acting and speaking as if they were the servants either of England or of France, Washington maintained his impartiality, and saw to it that the United States was kept out of European disputes. What was the result? He saved the country from fearful disaster; for he was like the pilot that conducts the ship through rapids and past dangerous reefs. But he himself suffered incredible contumely and reviling from the hot-headed partisans who were ready to plunge the country into the dispute. "If ever a nation," said one newspaper, "was debauched by a man, the American nation has been debauched by Washington. If ever a nation was deceived by a man, the American nation has been deceived by Washington. Let his conduct, then, be an example to future ages; let it serve to be a warning that no man may be an idol; let the history of the federal government instruct mankind that the mask of patriotism may be worn to conceal the foulest designs against the liberties of the people." That is the way some people wrote about Washington when he was president.

CHAPTER XXV.

THE FAREWELL.

WHEN Washington had completed his two terms of office, he was unalterably fixed in his resolution to go back to private life. The reasons which had induced him to accept the presidency against his inclination were no longer forcible. The government was established. The country was on the road to prosperity. No one man any longer had it in his power greatly to help or greatly to hurt the people. Moreover he was weary of public life. He was tired of standing up and being pelted with mud by all sorts of obscure people; of having his motives misconstrued; of listening to the endless bickerings of public men about him. For more than twenty years he had really been at the head of the nation. Now he meant to go back to his farm; but before he went, he had it in him to say one word to his countrymen.

That Washington should write his famous "Farewell Address to the People of the United States" indicates how accurately he understood his position. He was a great man, a splendid figure in history, and he knew it. But he was too great to be vain of his distinction. He was not too great to use even his distinction for the benefit of his country. He knew perfectly well that any speech which he might make when he retired from office would be listened to as almost no other political paper was ever listened to by a people, and he determined to gather into his "Farewell Address" the weightiest judgment which he could pronounce, as summing up the result of his long study and observation of public affairs. He wrote, of course, with a special eye to the needs of the people who were immediately to hear and read the address. They had dangers about them which have since largely disappeared; for example, we do not especially need to-day the caution which the men of that day needed when Washington wrote: "A passionate attachment of one nation for another produces a variety of evils."

Nevertheless, the address is so full of sound political wisdom that I wish it might be read in every public school in the land on the 22d day of February. In it the large-minded Washington speaks, thinking of the whole country, and pouring into his words the ripe and full judgment of a man whose one thought in his life had been to serve his country faithfully.

The observance of Washington's birthday began in a quiet way during Washington's lifetime. As early as 1783, when the war was over, but before the treaty of peace was signed, some gentlemen met together to celebrate it, and during his presidency, the day was observed by members of Congress and others who paid their respects to him, and the observance of the day became more and more general, especially after Washington's death.

The day before he was to leave office, Washington gave a farewell dinner to the Foreign Ministers and their wives, and eminent public men, including the new President, John Adams. The company was in excellent spirits, until Washington raised his glass to wish them all good health, after the fashion of those days. He smiled and said: "Ladies and gentlemen, this is the last time I shall drink your health as a public man; I do it with sincerity, wishing you all possible happiness." Perhaps he was thinking at the moment of his own happiness in going back to private life; but it suddenly rushed over the minds of those present what such a toast meant, and all mirth was gone. The next day he attended the ceremonies of the inauguration of John Adams. As he moved toward the door to retire, there was a rush of the people toward him. They cheered and cheered as he passed into the street. He answered, smiling and waving his hat, his gray hairs blown by the wind. The people followed him to the door of his house. He turned, as he entered, and looked on them. Now it was his place to feel the pain of parting. After all, he was going away from those busy haunts where he was sure to see men who honored and loved him. Tears stood in his eyes; his face was pale and grave; he raised his hand, but he could not trust himself to speak.

He was once more at Mount Vernon, in the quiet of his home, and again the days went by in that regular routine which suited him. Here is a letter which he wrote to James McHenry, the secretary of war: —

".I am indebted to you for several unacknowledged letters; but never mind that; go on as if you had answers. You are at the source of information, and can find many things to relate; while I have nothing to say that could either inform or amuse a secretary of war in Philadelphia. I might tell him that I begin my diurnal course with the sun; that, if my hirelings are not in their places at that time I send them messages of sorrow for their indisposition; that, having put these wheels in motion, I examine the state of things further; that, the more they are probed, the deeper I find the wounds which my buildings have sustained by an absence and neglect of eight years; that, by the time I have accomplished these matters, breakfast (a little after seven o'clock, about the time, I presume, you are taking leave of Mrs. McHenry) is ready; that, this being over, I mount my horse and ride round my farms, which employs me until it is time to dress for dinner, at which I rarely miss seeing strange faces, come, as they say, out of respect for me. Pray, would not the word curiosity answer as well? And how different this from having a few social friends at a cheerful board! The usual time of sitting at table, a walk, and tea, bring me within the dawn of candle light; previous to which, if not prevented by company, I resolve that, as soon as the glimmering taper supplies the place of the great luminary, I will retire to my writing-table and acknowledge the letters I have received; but when the lights are brought, I feel tired and disinclined to engage in this work, conceiving that the next night will do as well. The next night comes, and with it the same causes for postponement, and so on. This will account for your letter remaining so long unacknowledged; and, having given you the history of a day, it will serve for a year, and I am persuaded you will not require a second edition of it. But it may strike you that in this detail no mention is made of any portion of time allotted for reading. The remark would be just, for I have not looked into a book since I came home; nor shall I be able to do it until I have discharged my workmen, probably not before the nights grow longer, when possibly I may be looking in Doomsday Book. At present I shall only add that I am always and affectionately yours."

But the time came when a letter to the secretary of war was not a piece of pleasantry. There was imminent danger of war with France; Congress issued an order to raise an army, and President John Adams immediately nominated George Washington as commander-in-chief. The Senate promptly confirmed the nomination, and Washington accepted on two conditions: that the principal officers should be such as he approved, and that he should not be called into the field till the army required his presence. He did not think there would be war, but he believed the best way to prevent it was to show that the people were ready for it.

It was in March, 1797, that Washington left Philadelphia for Mount Vernon; in July, 1798, he was appointed commander-in-chief. He conducted most of his business by letter, though he spent a month in Philadelphia. He took up again the burden he had laid down, quietly, readily, since it was necessary, and without complaint; but he had not very long to bear it.

On December 12, 1799, he had been riding over his farms as usual, but a rain and sleet storm came up, and he returned to the house chilled through by the exposure. The next day was still stormy, and he kept indoors; but he had taken cold and suffered from a sore throat. He passed the evening with his family, however, read the papers, and talked cheerfully. In the night he had an attack of ague, and on the next morning, which was Saturday, the 14th, he breathed with difficulty, and messengers were sent for one doctor after another. He suffered acutely, but did not complain. Toward evening he said to Dr. Craik: "I die hard, but I am not afraid to die. I believed from my first attack that I should not survive it. My breath cannot last long." He said little more, only thanked his attendants for their kindness, and bade them give themselves no further trouble, —

simply to let him die in quietness. Between ten and eleven o'clock that night he died.

Chief Justice Marshall, when the news reached Congress, said a few simple words in the House of Representatives, and asked that a committee be appointed in conjunction with a committee of the Senate " to consider on the most suitable manner of paying honor to the memory of the man, *first in war, first in peace, and first in the hearts of his fellow-citizens ;* " but no manner has been found more suitable than the study of that life which is the most priceless gift to America.

INDEX.

ADAMS, John, proposes G.W. as commander-in-chief of the American army, 142, 143; coolness toward G. W., 179; presides at G. W.'s inauguration, 227; succeeds G. W. as president, 244.
Adams, Samuel, 134.
Annapolis, the scene of Washington's resignation, 210.

Belvoir, the Fairfax plantation, 39.
Birthday of G. W., 243.
Bishop, Billy, body-servant to G. W., 107; finds his master in no hurry, 108; how he cared for G. W.'s horses, 233.
Boston, siege of, 152-155.
Bouquet, Colonel, 105.
Braddock, Major-General Edward, put in command of all the forces, 84; arrives in Virginia, 85; invites G. W. to join his military family, 86; his character, 88; his conduct of the campaign, 89; makes his fatal blunder, 91; dies and is buried, 93.
Brandywine, battle of the, 170.
Bridge Creek, scene of G. W.'s school-days, 29.
Bunker Hill, effect of the battle of, on G. W., 146.
Burgoyne defeated by Gates, 170.

Cambridge Common, 149.
Chamberlayne, Mr., brings G. W. and Martha Custis together, 107, 108.
Clinton, General, succeeds General Howe, 187; fights the battle of Monmouth, 189; kept in New York, 198.
Cochran, Doctor, G. W.'s letter to, 195.
Concord, fight at, 140.
Congress issues the declaration of independence, 156; approves G. W.'s course in his encounter with Lord Howe, 160; puts full power into G. W.'s hands, 169; its vacillation, 173; reproached by G. W., 175; its inefficiency, 194; withholds pay from the soldiers, 204; its inability to meet the crisis after the war, 219.
Constitutional convention, 221-224.
Continental Congress, the First, 131-135; the second, 140-143.
Conway cabal, the, 178-186.
Cornwallis, Lord, crowded by General Greene, 198; at Yorktown, 199; surrenders to G. W., 201.
Craik, Dr., 247.
Custis, John, 109.
Custis, John Parke, 108.
Custis, Martha, afterwards Martha Washington, 108.

Declaration of Independence, 156.
Delaware, crossing the, 168.
Dinwiddie, Robert, 60; selects G. W. for a delicate mission, 63; orders G. W. on a foolhardy expedition, 81; his character, 100; G. W.'s difficulties with him, 101; is supplanted, 103.
Dorchester Heights, 154.
Duer, William, ready to vote, 133.

England, attitude of G. W. toward, 126.
English in America, the, 52; their relations with the Indians, 53; their activity in the Ohio valley, 53.

Fairfax, Anne, marries Lawrence Washington, 38.
Fairfax, George William, friend and companion of G. W., 40, 44.
Fairfax, Thomas, Lord, romantic life of, 41; his fondness for hunting, 42; gives G. W. a commission to survey his lands, 43; his life at Greenway Court, 48; dies, 49; G. W. turns to him for counsel, 81.
Fairfax, William, governor and planter, 39; his estate, 39.
Farewell address, the, 243.

INDEX.

Forbes, General, 103.
Fort Duquesne, 72, 91, 92; new movement against, 103; deserted by the French, 106.
Fort le Bœuf, 65.
Fort Necessity, 75, 77, 79, 93.
France, alliance of, with the United States, 170, 177.
Franklin, Benjamin, G. W. meets, for the first time, 88; meets him again at the Constitutional Convention, 222.
French in America, the, 52; their relations with the Indians, 53; their activity in the Ohio valley, 53; build a fort on English territory, 61; defeat Braddock, 91; driven from the Ohio valley, 106.
Fry, Joshua, 71, 76.

Gage, General, and his nose, 151.
Gates, General, in the Conway cabal, 180, 182, 185.
Gist, Christopher, accompanies G. W. on his expedition to the Ohio, 63; makes a perilous journey with him, 66.
Great Meadows, 73; battle of, 78, 93.
Greene, General Nathanael, 150; in command at Fort Lee, 167.
Greenway Court, Lord Fairfax's quarters, 48.
Grimes, Miss, the young lady who did not marry G. W., 36.

Hamilton, Alexander, 224; made secretary of the treasury, 229.
Harvard College, 148.
Henry, Patrick, 131, 134, 139.
Hite, Captain, 45.
Hobby, the sexton, who taught G. W. to read, 23.
Howe, Admiral, 156.
Howe, Lord, 157; tries in vain to avoid calling Washington general, 157; presses G. W., 165; turns the army over to Clinton, 187.

Indian dress, approved by G. W. for his troops, 104.

Jefferson, Thomas, 229.
Jumonville, Ensign, 74.

Kalb, Baron, 185.
Knox, General, 200; bids G. W. good-by, 209.

La Fayette, Marquis de, joins the American army, 184; rebukes the Conway party, 185; at Monmouth, 189; reproduces the Newburgh headquarters in Paris, 203.
Lear, Tobias, G. W.'s secretary, 237.
Lee, General Charles, appearance of, 149; at White Plains, 167; his conduct in New Jersey, 168; opposes active measures, 188; his conduct at Monmouth, 189-192; is court-martialled, 193.
Lee, Richard Henry, early correspondence of, with G. W., 23.
Lee, Thomas, founder of the Ohio Company, 54.
Lexington, battle of, 140.
Livingston, Robert R., 227.
Long Island, battle of, 161.

McHenry, James, letter of G. W. to, 245.
Mackay, Captain, 76, 78.
Mackenzie, Captain, 136.
Marshall, Chief Justice John, his famous words on G. W., 248.
Mason, George, 117.
Mifflin, General, in the Conway cabal, 178, 181, 186.
Monmouth, battle of, 189.
Morris, Gouverneur, 183, 184.
Muse, Major, teaches G. W. the art of war, 56.

Newburgh, headquarters at, 203; reproduced by La Fayette in Paris, 203.
New England and Virginia, 141-143.

Ohio Company, the, 54; its origin and purpose, 54; fostered by the Washingtons, 55; concerned in the movements of the French, 62; proposes to build a fort, 64.

Patterson, Colonel, 159.
Pendleton, Edmund, 131.
Pitt, William, at the head of affairs, 103.
Pittsburgh, the beginning of, 72.
Planters, Virginia, and their life, 13-20; as illustrated by G. W., 110-114.
Pohick Church, 118.
Princeton, battle of, 169.
Profanity rebuked by G. W., 161.
Provoost, Bishop, 228.

Reed, Colonel, refuses to receive a letter, 158.
Robinson, Mr. Speaker, his little speech, 121.
Rochambeau, Count, 199.

INDEX.

Rules of Civility and Decent Behavior in Company and Conversation, 31.

St. Clair, General, warned by G. W. before fighting the Indians, 236; how G. W. received the news of his defeat, 237.
Sainte Pierre, M. de, 66.
Schuyler, Major-General Philip, 146.
Sharpe, Governor, of Maryland, 83; offers G. W. a commission, 84.
Shingiss, a friendly Indian, 64.
Shippen, Dr., 133.
Shirley, Governor, 100; G. W. consults him, 100, 132.
Slaves, the first, in Virginia, 11; their life, 15, 16; under G. W., 113.
Stamp Act, the, 122.
Stephen, Colonel, 119.
Steuben, Baron, inspector of the army, 177.
Stirling, Lord, 181.

Taxes, imposition of, by Parliament, 127.
Tobacco, the great Virginian product, 9; used as currency, 12; fields of, 15.
Trent, Captain, 70, 72.
Trenton, battle of, 169.
Truro parish, 117.

Valley Forge, winter quarters at, 170; preparation for the camp at, 171; privations of the men at, 172; the terrible winter at, 175.
Van Braam, Jacob, gives G. W. lessons in sword exercise, 56; accompanies him as interpreter, 63; at the battle of Great Meadows, 78.
Varick, Colonel Richard, puts G. W.'s papers in order, 212.
Vernon, Admiral, Lawrence Washington serves under, 37, 38; his name given to Mount Vernon, 38.
Vernon, Mount, the Washington house at, 38; its neighbors, 39; the home of G. W., 51; in peril of marauders, 197.
Virginia, the old boundaries of, 7; its water ways, 8; absence of large towns in, 8; capital of, 8; the most populous colony in America, 9; occupations of the people in, 9; the great estates of, 10; the colonists to, 10; indentured servants in, 11; the beginning of African slavery in, 11; the tobacco planting in, 12; plantation life in, 13-20; divided into parishes, 21; the soldiers of, at Braddock's defeat, 92, 93; the life of, as affecting military service, 99; the loyalty of G. W. toward, 125; its attitude before the war, 139; G. W.'s plans for it after the war, 217.

Ward, Ensign, 72.
Ward, General Artemas, 149.
Washington, Augustine, father of George, 21; removes to Stafford County, 22; death of, 24.
Washington, Augustine, half brother of George, 22; marries and makes a home for G. W., 29; is interested in the Ohio Company, 62.
Washington, George, parents of, 21; born, 22; learns to read, 23; holds correspondence with R. H. Lee, 23; influenced by his mother, 25, 26; breaks colt, 27; his athletic sports, 28; makes his home with his brother Augustine, 29; goes to school to Mr. Williams, 30; his exercise books, 30, 31; the rules he copied, 31, 32; plays at soldiering, 33; gets a warrant as midshipman, 34; is prevented from serving by his mother and uncle, 34, 35; studies surveying, 35; has a boyish love affair, 36; under the charge of his brother Lawrence, 37; a guest at Belvoir, 40; his friendship with the Fairfaxes, 40-44; sets out on a surveying excursion, 45; his first experience of roughing it, 46; falls in with Indians, 47; keeps a diary, 47; is made public surveyor, 50; lays the foundation of his success, 50; his self-reliance and his studies, 51; becomes adjutant-general, 55; goes through a military training, 56; goes to West Indies with his brother Lawrence, 56; takes small-pox, 57; his early habits of order and economy, 58; returns to Virginia, 59; an executor of his brother's estate, 59; made major, 60; sent as commissioner to the French, 62; reaches Cumberland, 63; holds a council with the Indians, 65; pushes forward to Fort le Bœuf, 65; his perilous return journey, 66-68; raises a company for frontier work, 70; made lieutenant-colonel, 71; reaches Wills Creek, 72; camps at Great Meadows, 73; surprises the enemy, 74; rears Fort Necessity, 75; divides command with Captain Mackay, 76; offers fight at Great Meadows, 77; is defeated, 78; his first Fourth of July, 79; receives a vote of thanks, 80; ordered to make

252 INDEX.

a fresh expedition, 81; protests in a letter to Lord Fairfax, 81; resigns his commission, 83; has an offer from Governor Sharpe of Maryland, 83, 84; addresses General Braddock, 85; is appointed aid-de-camp, 86; joins the expedition, 87; takes part in the councils, 89; suffers from ill health, 90; cautions Braddock, 91; in the heat of battle, 93; returns to Mount Vernon, 94; is made commander-in-chief of the Virginia forces, 95; encounters great difficulties in the matter of men and supplies, 96, 97; labors over the matter of discipline, 98; makes a journey to Boston to consult with Governor Shirley, 100; his trying position, 101; undertakes an expedition against Fort Duquesne, 103; advises an Indian dress, 104; resigns his commission again, 106; is sent for to advise the Quartermaster-General, 107; stops at Mr. Chamberlayne's, 107; makes a long stay at dinner, 108; falls promptly in love with Mrs. Custis, 108; takes his wife and her children by a former marriage to Mount Vernon, 109; his life as a Virginia planter, 110, 111; his management of his property, 111, 112; his relation to slavery, 113; his hospitality, 114; his love of sport, 115; his contradiction of character, 116; a vestryman, 117; draws plans for Pohick Church, 118; elected a member of the House of Burgesses, 120; the character of his civil work, 121; his views on the Stamp Act, 123; his relations with England, 124; his citizenship in Virginia, 125; his loyalty, 126; his patriotic position, 128; appointed delegate to the first Continental Congress, 130; starts for Philadelphia, 131; his speech at Williamsburg, 132; lodges at Dr. Shippen's, 133; effect produced by him on the convention, 134; becomes acquainted with people, 135; his letter to Captain Mackenzie, 136; a delegate to a second Virginia convention, 138; delegate to the second Continental Congress, 140; nominated commander-in-chief of the American army, 142; writes to his wife on the subject, 144; leaves Philadelphia for the north, 146; is welcomed by the Provincial Congress at Watertown, 147; takes possession of what afterward became the Longfellow house, 148; draws his sword at the head of the army, 149; his first duties, 151; drives the British from Boston, 154; becomes the great leader, 155; in New York, 156; Mr. W. or Gen. W.? 157; his order against profanity, 161; withdraws his army after the battle of Long Island, 162; occupies White Plains, 165; retreats before the British army, 167; crosses the Delaware, 168; is given full power, 169; prevents the British from moving on Philadelphia, 170; fights the battle of the Brandywine and goes into winter quarters at Valley Forge, 170; bravely encourages his men, 171; reproaches Congress, 175; how he carried himself, 176; at prayer, 176; his use of Steuben, 177; the intrigue of the Conway party against him, 178; rebukes Gates, 180; his brief letter to Conway, 181; his friendship for La Fayette, 184; his frustration of his enemies' plans, 186; sets off after Clinton's army, 187; is checked by Lee, 188; rebukes Lee, 191; orders a court-martial after Monmouth, 193; his army dinner, 195; indifference to his private interests, 197; visits Mount Vernon, 198; brings Cornwallis to bay, 199; his coolness under fire, 200; escorts his mother to a ball, 201; establishes headquarters at Newburgh, 203; his reception of a proposal to make him dictator, 205; redresses the wrongs of the army, 207; studies the great question of government, 208; takes leave of his brother officers, 209; renders his accounts, 210; resigns his commission, 211; retires to Mount Vernon, 212; looks after his estate, 213; in the hands of painters and sculptors, 214; his attitude toward the young, 215; his hospitality, 216; makes a tour beyond the Alleghanies, 217; his large plans for Virginia, 218; a member of the Constitutional Convention, 221; calls on Benjamin Franklin, 222; presides over the convention, 222; his attitude toward the Constitution, 223; is chosen President, 225; his triumphal progress to New York, 226; is inaugurated, 227, 228; his administration of office, 229; his extraordinary industry, 230; his notion of civil service, 231; his social habits, 232; his recreation, 233; his regard for Mount Vernon, 235; makes tours, 236; his reception of the news of St. Clair's defeat, 237–239; the hostility shown him, 241; delivers his farewell address, 242; takes leave of public life, 244; is recalled by the danger of war with France, 246; is taken ill, 247; dies, 248.

Washington, John, grandfather of George, 21.

Washington, Lawrence, half brother of George, 22; sent to England to be educated, 37; serves under Admiral Vernon, 38; marries Anne Fairfax, 38; lives at Mount Vernon, 38; manager of the Ohio Company, 55; goes to Barbadoes, 56; dies, 59.

Washington, Martha, a glimpse of, in her old age, 20; her marriage, 109; in camp with G. W., 176; receives with G. W., 232; her domestic tastes, 234.

Washington, Mary, the mother of G. W., the character of, 24, 25; how addressed by her son, 25; refuses to let G. W. go into the navy, 34; joins G. W. after the battle of Yorktown, 201.

Webster, Noah, 147.

White Plains, battle of, 166.

Williams, Mr., G. W.'s schoolmaster, 30.

Williamsburg, the capital of Virginia, 8, 18.

Wright, Mr., models G. W.'s face, 214.

Yorktown, surrender of Cornwallis at, 199.